A Brave N

GLOBAL
IN A CHANG

C000148824

This series of short, accessible
ing global issues of relevance
for the enquiring reader and social activists in the North and
the South, as well as students, the books explain what is at
stake and question conventional ideas and policies. Drawn
from many different parts of the world, the series' authors
pay particular attention to the needs and interests of ordinary
people, whether living in the rich industrial or the developing
countries. They all share a common objective: to help stimulate
new thinking and social action in the opening years of the
new century.

Global Issues in a Changing World is a joint initiative by Zed
Books in collaboration with a number of partner publishers
and non-governmental organizations around the world. By
working together, we intend to maximize the relevance and
availability of the books published in the series.

Participating NGOs

Both ENDS, Amsterdam
Catholic Institute for International Relations, London
Corner House, Sturminster Newton
Council on International and Public Affairs, New York
Dag Hammarskjöld Foundation, Uppsala
Development GAP, Washington DC
Focus on the Global South, Bangkok
IBON, Manila
Inter Pares, Ottawa
Public Interest Research Centre, Delhi
Third World Network, Penang
Third World Network–Africa, Accra
World Development Movement, London

About this series

Communities in the South are facing great difficulties in coping with global trends. I hope this brave new series will throw much-needed light on the issues ahead and help us choose the right options.

Martin Khor, Director, Third World Network, Penang

There is no more important campaign than our struggle to bring the global economy under democratic control. But the issues are fearsomely complex. This Global Issues series is a valuable resource for the committed campaigner and the educated citizen.

Barry Coates, Director, Oxfam New Zealand

Zed Books has long provided an inspiring list about the issues that touch and change people's lives. The Global Issues series is another dimension of Zed's fine record, allowing access to a range of subjects and authors that, to my knowledge, very few publishers have tried. I strongly recommend these new, powerful titles and this exciting series.

John Pilger, author

We are all part of a generation that actually has the means to eliminate extreme poverty worldwide. Our task is to harness the forces of globalization for the benefit of working people, their families and their communities – that is our collective duty. The Global Issues series makes a powerful contribution to the global campaign for justice, sustainable and equitable development, and peaceful progress.

Glenys Kinnock MEP

About this book

The world of international mining is changing rapidly. Mining corporations are encroaching on more and more greenfield sites in Africa, the Asia-Pacific and Latin America, to serve ever-expanding global industries. Roger Moody shows that large-scale mining imposes a heavy toll on local communities, on their fragile economies and ways of life, as well as the environment. He challenges the mining corporations' recent public relations offensive extolling the virtues of large-scale mining and its alleged compatibility with sustainable development, and reveals the unprecedented wave of community and trade union opposition to projects in both the South and the North. This important book concludes with urgent proposals to check the role of multinationals in a sector that has always been at the core of resource exploitation.

About the author

Roger Moody is Managing Editor of the Mines and Communities website. He is an experienced international researcher and campaigner who has travelled extensively, particularly in the Asia-Pacific region. As an activist he has worked with community organizations in South America, the Asia-Pacific and Africa. He has been keynote speaker at numerous conferences on mining, including the World Council of Churches consultation on mining and indigenous peoples (1996), Third World Africa's conference on the social and environmental impacts of mining (2000) and more recently, the World Social Forum, Mumbai, on the global impacts of mining (2004). Among his many works are the highly acclaimed *The Gulliver File: Mines, People and Land – A Global Battleground* (Minewatch/WISE Glen Aplin/International Books, 1992), *The Indigenous Voice: Visions and Realities* (Zed Books, 1988) and his most recent work, *The Risks We Run: Mining, Communities and Political Risk Insurance* (International Books, Utrecht, 2005).

ROGER MOODY

Rocks and hard places

The globalization of mining

Fernwood Publishing
NOVA SCOTIA

Books *for* Change
BANGALORE

SIRD
KUALA LUMPUR

David Philip
CAPE TOWN

Zed Books
LONDON | NEW YORK

Rocks and hard places: the globalization of mining was first published in 2007, by:

in Canada: Fernwood, 32 Oceanvista Lane, Site 2A, Box 5, Black Point, Nova Scotia BOJ 1BO

in India: Books *for* Change, 139 Richmond Road, Bangalore 560 025, Karnataka

in Malaysia: Strategic Information Research Department (SIRD), No. 11/4E, Petaling Jaya, 46200 Selangor

in Southern Africa: David Philip Publishers (Pty Ltd), 99 Garfield Road, Claremont 7700, South Africa

in the rest of the world: Zed Books Ltd, 7 Cynthia Street, London N1 9JF, UK and Room 400, 175 Fifth Avenue, New York, NY 10010, USA

www.zedbooks.co.uk

Cover designed by Andrew Corbett
Set in Arnhem and Futura Bold by Ewan Smith, London
Index by <ed.emery@thefreeuniversity.net>
Printed and bound in Malta by Gutenberg Press Ltd

Distributed in the USA exclusively by Palgrave Macmillan, a division of St Martin's Press, LLC, 175 Fifth Avenue, New York, NY 10010

A catalogue record for this book is available from the British Library
US CIP data are available from the Library of Congress

Library and Archives Canada Cataloguing in Publication
Moody, Roger
Rocks and hard places : the new world of global mining / Roger Moody.
(Global issues series)
Includes bibliographical references and index.
ISBN 978-1-55266-233-5
    1. Mines and mineral resources--Environmental aspects. 2. Mines and mineral resources--Social aspects. 3. Mines and mineral resources--Political aspects. 4. Mines and mineral resources--Economic aspects. I. Title. II. Series: Global issues (Halifax, N.S.)
    TD195.M5M65 2006   333.8'516   C2006-906204-8

ISBN 978 1 84277 174 7 hb (Zed Books)
ISBN 978 1 84277 175 4 pb (Zed Books)
ISBN 978 1 55266 233 5 (Fernwood Publishing)

Contents

Boxes

Acknowledgements

My thanks go to Richard, Whit, Helen and
Mickie for their personal support; to Robert at
Zed for the initial invitation and to Susannah
at Zed for her exceptional forbearance; and to
Alex and Alan for teaching me more than they
were probably aware.

Also, my gratitude to Felix Padel for the cover
photo, which depicts working conditions at
Vedanta Resources' Bodai-Daldali bauxite mine
in mid 2006.

1 | Through the minefield

Twenty years ago, when researching RTZ (then the world's biggest mining company), I was struck by a curious anomaly. All three chief architects of the company between 1954 and the late eighties had listed 'gardening' as a favoured pursuit in *Who's Who*, the UK dictionary of biographies. Here were these captains of a highly dangerous and destructive industry regularly retiring to their rose beds, even as (as I knew full well) their company was conniving with the apartheid and Pinochet regimes; violating a United Nations decree forbidding extraction of Namibia's natural resources; and turning an entire Australian Aboriginal home land into a 'moonscape'. How did they sleep at night? Would they one day be compelled to face their accusers and confess their sins, or simply take to their spades and forks, muttering (if pressed) that they 'didn't know' what was going on?

A lot of water has gone down many rivers since that research was completed in 1991.[1] But so has an awful lot of toxic junk. More than 200,000 tonnes of it still plunge daily into the Ajkwa river system of West Papua from the Grasberg copper-gold mine, responsibility for which Rio Tinto (as RTZ is now known) shares with Freeport of the USA. Until the dawn of the new century, some 120 community, workers' and NGO representatives had turned up at various Rio Tinto annual shareholders' meetings, to recite a litany of its derelictions and deceit, usually backed by solid documentary evidence. All of them went away bitterly disappointed.

Now Rio Tinto presents a very different image to a significantly different audience. Several well-known environmental groups consider the company to lead the 'natural resources extraction' sector (an inadequate term that's none the less become synony-mous with mining and mineral processing) by offering up 'multi-stakeholder partnerships' and an ever-rolling log of 'dialogues' with sceptics. Then United Nations Secretary-General Kofi Annan was certainly grateful for the support Rio Tinto gave him when he launched the Global Compact in 1999 to 'lead the world in promoting corporate social responsibility'. Three years later the British prime minister proffered Rio's chairman, Robert Wilson, a warm handshake for helping launch the Extractive Industries Transparency Initiative (EITI) at the second World Summit for Sustainable Development. All these, however, were outmatched by Rio Tinto's biggest public relations achievement, the estab-lishment of the Global Mining Initiative (GMI) in 1999. This spawned the Mining, Minerals and Sustainable Development (MMSD) study project, which is probably the broadest-scoped critical examination of an industrial sector yet performed. When MMSD segued into the International Council on Mining and Metals (ICMM) in October 2001 it was a triumph for the company and Robert Wilson in particular. Almost inevitably he became first chair of this new vanguard for the minerals industry (see Chapter 7).

But the disturbing fact remains that Rio Tinto has never apolo-gized for a single one of its misdeeds stretching back 130 years and on which its prowess as the most diversified of global miners is based. The nearest it has come to contrition was an expres-sion of vague regret for its stark neocolonial stripping of a huge copper-gold deposit on the Papua New Guinean island of Bou-gainville. Leased in 1966, when the territory was under Australian control, within six years the Panguna mine had become the most commercially successful of all the company's operations. Costs were savagely cut by dumping all the mine's wastes (tailings) into the nearby river. By 1988 a few of the Panguna indigenous landowners, led by a former Rio Tinto mineworker, Francis Ona, demanded US$10 billion compensation for the ruination of their gardens, forests and waterways. The company jeered at the claim and refused to negotiate. Ona set up a nucleonic 'Bougainville Revolutionary Army', declaring independence from Papua New Guinea. Backed by Australian helicopter gunships, troops from the mainland invaded the island. In the bloody civil war that ensued up to a fifth of the island's population (between 15,000 and 20,000 villagers, many of them women and children) were to die before peace was reached in early 1998.[2] Rio Tinto belatedly confessed that it could have 'done things otherwise' regarding Bougainville and, over the succeeding eight years, broadly hinted that it would never resume mining on the island. Then, in 2006, as copper and gold prices reached a record high, rumours began spreading through the mining media that the company was planning a possible return.[3]

Rio Tinto's self-promotion as the mining industry's 'benchmarker' for sustainable development has gained it entry to numerous, mainly European, conferences on 'ethical investment' that these days fall upon our heads like confetti. It is a very different story for scores of communities and many trade unionists – from Australia to Zimbabwe – who continue viewing the company with the deepest suspicion. But it isn't only Rio Tinto which faces such antagonism, although in recent years the company has attracted more grassroots opprobrium than any other. These days every big mining company vigorously pushes its own envelope on 'improved practices' and 'transparency' while having to face serious accusations that it fails to respect cultures, protect the environment and return fair shares of its profits to the countries where it operates. As I write this, my desk is cluttered with alerts and alarums. CVRD, the Brazil iron ore giant, is about to sue Xikrin tribespeople for 'invading' what is actually their own ancestral land, stolen from them twenty years before.[4] The Canadian government is now permitting miners to

3

use freshwater lakes on First Nation (native peoples') lands in which to dump toxic wastes.[5] Inco, the world's second-biggest nickel producer, is building a smelter in New Caledonia, despite a court order obtained by local Kanaks prohibiting the company from doing so.[6]

So is all this talk about industry reform, with which we're now regularly regaled, a sham? The answer is both 'yes' and 'no'. BHPBilliton has vowed never again to use rivers or oceans for disposal of its tailings, and the odds are that it will not. (The international outcry would be deafening, and local reaction verge towards sabotage.) But BHPBilliton, the world's leading 'diversified resources' resources corporation, has also said it will refrain from mining in 'protected areas', and that particular promise must be strongly doubted (see Chapter 8). Three years ago, in the wake of an international campaign by the Aboriginal Mirrar people of northern Australia which included sending a spokeswoman to the company's annual general meeting, Rio Tinto pledged not to enter their traditional territory without obtaining their consent.[7] If the Mirrar remain strong and united then the company will hardly dare break the agreement. Several years ago, however, Rio Tinto also promised not to invest in Burma while the vicious regime was still in power. The US gold miner Newmont had just been forced to withdraw from the country under threat of US sanctions. But then, in October 2006, Rio pledged up to US$1.7 billion to a 'junior' miner, called Ivanhoe, in order to access a huge copper lode in Mongolia. Ivanhoe also mines Burmese copper in a fifty-fifty partnership with the military. The UK company had broken its word.[8]

In the following pages I seek to separate out obfuscation from reality, primarily from the perspectives of those most affected by both big and small mining: those who have seen their own resources sequestered or tainted by a mine or processing plant and the workers hired to operate them. It has not been an easy

4

task for vital data are often lacking. How many children, for example, are affected by the worst effects of quarrying – the most pervasive, but least publicized, of extractive endeavours (see Chapter 5)? Is it a few million or tens of millions? We do not know for certain. Nor can we be sure of the precise impacts of many recent tailings' dam bursts or cyanide 'spills' (see Chapter 6), though vigorously asserting that they should never have been allowed to happen. A gaggle of 'experts' will often be on hand offering up wildly conflicting versions of what a 'mine development plan' will mean in practice. Whom to believe? From long experience I know that, after metaphorically 'going down the mine' to seek out the truth, one often returns to the surface with more questions than answers.

Defining sustainability

Nevertheless, some basic realities cannot be disputed. All metals and minerals are finite, many created within the earth's crust by unrepeatable geophysical events of a billion or more years ago. Once they are uprooted then processed they cannot be returned to their original state. Nor can we exactly replace, or leave undisturbed, the earth, rocks, sands, rivers or oceans that hosted these deposits. It is true that metals may be recycled and often are – though rarely to their full potential. (Ironically more scrap aluminium is likely to be retrieved from the streets and waste dumps of Brazil than those of New York or Tokyo.) Many metallic objects common to everyday life could be passed between us almost indefinitely – but too few are. The World Gold Council, an industry body, is keen to tell us (through its new 'Trust Gold' campaign) that the metal is essential to electronics, computers, mobile phones, dentistry and certain alloys. The Council is less ready to point out that around 90 per cent of gold ever mined is theoretically available for reuse. In principle there is no reason to extract a single ounce more gold for utilitarian

5

purposes. The metal is, however, stored in bank vaults and rests in (or literally on) private hands. Only a transformation of the global monetary system, and a puncturing of the mythologies woven around gold's virtues as a 'store of value' and a 'hedge against inflation', are likely to change that.

Nor should we chant 'Recycle and Reuse!' as if this were a hallowed mantra. Melting down scrap metals exerts its own ecological price in terms of further sulphur dioxide and carbon dioxide emissions and discharges of chemical wastes. Recycled goods rarely circulate back among those whose land has offered up the vital raw materials in the first place. When they do, the monetary gains from reprocessing tend (like those from primary extraction) to end up in foreign pockets. Savings in energy and labour made through secondary processing rarely get reflected in lower market prices to those South-based consumers.

Whatever the justifications for digging up more and more minerals, their stock is continually going down and the rate of depletion has been accelerating over many decades.[9] Natural resource extraction per se cannot be reconciled with long-term sustainability. For industry spokespeople to claim (as they often do) that there is such a thing as 'sustainable mining' is a transparent oxymoron. Nevertheless, whether mining can contribute to 'sustainable development' through providing jobs, paying taxes, building infrastructure and funding ancillary social services is another question.

All of us depend on metals and minerals to varying extents for power, transport, infrastructure, housing, grey and white consumer goods. Recycling and reusing them will never match with needs so long as what we sometimes glibly call 'rising social expectations' fail to be satisfied. The rapid burgeoning of a middle class in China and India – fast approaching three-quarters of a billion people – makes increased demand for raw materials inevitable. It is a key factor contributing to recent industry plans to encroach upon, and under, the Arctic, dig into the deep sea bed, and even prospect for minerals on the moon and other planets.[10] The pressing question is therefore not 'do we mine or not mine?' Some minerals, especially those used in construction, will always be needed and some types of extraction will continue indefinitely.

Rather we have to ask ourselves: *what, how, when, where* – and *by whom* – is it acceptable to do so?

What to mine?

Very few metals have a unique application. Gold is so ductile that a gram of it can be stretched more than 3 kilometres, but the need to do so rarely arises. Uranium is the predominant raw source for manufacturing nuclear fuel but not the only one: thorium dug up from mineral (beach) sands may be used as well. Platinum is the commonest metal employed in catalytic converters, designed to limit noxious exhaust fumes from internal combustion engines. Manganese, nickel and iron can, however, be incorporated too. Even more important, there are potential substitutes for metals and other extracted materials available for a whole host of human endeavours, with the major exceptions of waging modern warfare and travelling long distances at great speed. 'Advances' made by our forebears may have seemed inevitable at the time (for example, changing from iron to copper, then copper to aluminium, in fashioning cooking pots). But they were determined by factors – availability of the raw material, technology to process it – which do not necessarily prevail today. We are now beginning – if far too slowly – to understand that there have been huge socio-economic and environmental penalties attached to making those earlier choices, in particular from burning coal and smelting heavy metals. Calculating the 'life-cycle costs' (energy consumed, wastes produced, pollution delivered) of transmuting a raw mined substance into a finished product is finally being recognized as a serious and necessary science. It is no longer just the preserve of isolated bands of hopeless idealists. There is a growing consensus that some mined substances are so dangerous they should never be taken from the ground. Asbestos in all its forms is banned in the USA and throughout the European Union. But, inexcusably, Canada and Russia continue selling stockpiles of the carcinogenic mineral across the world. Some South-based states (notably India) are now increasing their consumption of asbestos, predominantly for cement (see Chapter 5). Mercury, banned in 2006 by the European Union for use in thermometers, is still being dumped by European states in Africa and Asia in the form of 'e-wastes' (mostly discarded computers and mobile phones). Cement kilns and power utilities also put significant quantities of mercury into the air, not least in the USA. Clearly global trade in both these substances should be banned. But how do we evaluate the consequences of using (or misusing) other potentially deadly toxic heavy metals, notably lead, cadmium and nickel? Although it has long been discontinued in the manufacture of paint and piping, market demand for lead last year increased rather than diminished. Nickel, one of the most toxic of heavy metals, is being incorporated into batteries for hybrid cars claimed to be 'green'. Aluminium is promoted as a substitute for steel in automobiles, so as to reduce fuel consumption and thereby global greenhouse gas emissions (GGE). But aluminium refining and smelting itself gives rise to significant quantities of carbon dioxide and, tonne for tonne, is the largest industrial consumer of electricity.[11] Should our taxes be directed only at promoting and exporting 'renewable' energy? Or does coal currently bulwark so many fragile developing economies that we would do better funding 'clean coal mechanisms' – even though the efficiency of these is questionable? As pointed out by the *Mining Journal* last year: 'Thus far none of these [technologies] provides the "quick fix" solution that some parties to the Kyoto Protocol are hoping for.' China's own emissions of GGE and sulphur not only threaten millions of inhabitants of the mainland, but the whole of East Asia and those living as far afield as the west coast of North America.[12]

The how of it

Choosing the best method of extraction first of all requires distinguishing between dirty technologies and potentially less damaging ones. You may well come to share the opinions of many, reflected in this book, that it can never be justified to throw toxic mine wastes into rivers and seas, or spray cyanide on to ore to separate out gold (see Chapter 8). But an equally important question for many mining-impacted communities and workers is whether raw materials are excavated from underground shafts, open pits or 'stripped' from the earth's surface.

The first employs substantially more workers, but wreaks a higher toll in fatalities and occupational disease (see Chapter 4). On the other hand, open pit and strip mining take over much larger acreages of fertile land. Cement manufacturers are burning almost every conceivable type of industrial, chemical and agricultural waste in their kilns, to convert lime and gypsum into the 'glue' that holds together our buildings and infrastructure. Is this, as claimed, reducing the toll from GGE? Or does it pose new dangers? (see Chapter 5).

When to mine?

For some years the evidence has been growing that, if a 'lesser-developing' state relies heavily on income from mineral sales, it will add to, rather than subtract from, the continuing impoverishment of many of its citizens. What are the root causes of this so-called 'minerals curse': institutional failures (nepotism, corruption and inequitable distribution of internal revenues) which may be redressed by better governance? Or the savage emasculation of royalty and taxation regimes, largely imposed by the World Bank/IMF (see Chapter 2) and the intrinsic nature of a global commodities system where mineral exports are prized too highly above alternative items of production? The fundamental challenge, I believe, is to devise a truly humanist methodology which values mineral deposits before they get turned over by the drills and bulldozers then sent offshore. We have to set the long-term sociocultural and ecological consequences of mining against what might be gained from rents and other minerals-derived incomes in the present. Leaving the raw materials in the ground may prove the only way that many lesser-developing states can retain their diversities of real wealth, while there remains the option to resume mining at a later stage (see Chapter 3).

Where not *to go?*

Indigenous peoples are custodians of territories under which are some of the richest ores found on the planet. Their territories host the majority of reserves and resources currently targeted by companies and governments and many of these are also protected areas and biosphere reserves. By the time this book is published, the UN General Assembly will have considered for adoption and ratification the draft text of a 'Declaration on the Rights of Indigenous Peoples'. If accepted as a Final Declaration, the doors will have been inched open to a measure for which indigenous peoples have been struggling for many years. It affirms both their rights to self-determination and 'individual and collective land and resource rights'. States that ratify are bound to 'consult and cooperate in good faith with the indigenous peoples concerned through their own representative institutions in order to obtain their free and informed consent prior to the approval of any project affecting their lands or territories and other resources ...'. Canada and Russia voted against the draft, while Argentina, Ghana and the Philippines were among the heavily mineralized states, hosting a significant number of First Peoples, that abstained.[13] Whatever the outcome of the UN deliberations, the concept of 'fully informed prior consent' (FIPC) has already become central to current and putative negotiations between companies, governments and communities, over access to minerals on their territories (see Chapters 2 and 8). To date, the minerals industry has almost universally failed to recognize this right. But there are, I suggest, few other issues that strike so directly to the heart of contemporary debates about self-empowerment, the implementation of democracy and ultimately the sustainability of our planet.

Who should do the mining?

The majority of those who do our mining are not, as might be thought, employed by multinational corporations. Instead, they comprise millions of men and women – a large number indigenous themselves – whose tasks range from sluicing diamonds from tropical rivers in Latin America, working on large cooperative tin mining operations in Bolivia and hewing and hauling building materials in some of the most dangerous places on earth (see Chapter 5). Allegations against this so-called 'artisanal and small mining sector' occasionally hit the headlines in the shape of accusations that they are behind the peddling of 'blood' diamonds from west and central Africa, or poisoning themselves and the environment by burning mercury to extract gold. In comparison we learn hardly anything about the lives of millions of stone-breakers in South Asia or those who toil down thousands of illegal coal pits in China. All of them are trying to make a living, but many are also indirectly (if unwittingly) displacing unionized miners from their jobs, since increasing numbers of casual workers are now being subcontracted to big mining companies in order to cut costs (see Chapter 4). It is impossible to tell how much global mineral production can currently be ascribed to small-scale miners. But what surely cannot be denied is that the potential for democratic self-organization within thousands of mining communities is currently being squandered. It is one of the least visible but most insidious results of the inexorable concentration of power – both financial and political – in the hands of the world's big miners (see Box 1.1).

At the end of the day, and after weighing up the human and environmental consequences of that reality, we may be driven to one overwhelming conclusion: that decisions over the what, when, where, how and by whom of extracting irreplaceable mineral resources must no longer be entrusted to 'the industry'.

We rise up in alarm at the prospect of our rivers, lakes and oceans being privatized. But there is an equally compelling case to declare the world's minerals also to be the common heritage of humankind.

*Box 1.1 Corporate control over mines and minerals:
the top ten global miners*

Name	Headquarters	Market capitalization (in \$US billions)*
1) BHPBilliton	Australia/UK	109
2) Rio Tinto	UK/Australia	77
3) CVRD/Inco	Brazil/Canada	72
4) Anglo American	UK	56
5) Xstrata/Falcon -bridge	Switzerland/UK/ Canada	39
6) Alcoa	USA	26
7) Barrick/Placer	Canada	25
8) Newmont	USA	24
9) Norilsk	Russia	17
10) Phelps Dodge	USA	14

Note: * Rounded figures compiled from *Forbes Global 2000* and other sources. Exploration data are from the Metals Economics Group, Halifax, Nova Scotia.

The market capitalization of the world's ten biggest miners outmatches those of all other mining companies put together, and their most important single source of financing is the *London Stock Exchange* (LSE), followed by *Toronto's*. The majority of junior mining companies are also registered in Toronto, with significant listings in *Australia* and on *London's Alternative Investment Market* (AIM).

By far the most important *private investor* in mining is the *global commodities trader* Glencore, which, along with the Credit Suisse First Boston investment bank, also holds a 40 per cent equity interest in Xstrata/Falconbridge.

Exploration budgets reached their highest-ever level in 2006 (at US$7.13 billion). The most targeted metal was gold, then base metals such as copper, nickel and zinc. *Latin America* attracted nearly a quarter of all exploration funding (24 per cent), followed by *Canada* (19 per cent), *Africa* (16 per cent), *Australia* (11 per cent) , the *USA* (8 per cent) and the *Asia-Pacific* region (4 per cent).

Some examples of contemporary corporate control over minerals:

Coal In 2005 the biggest global producers were *Peabody Energy (USA)*, *Rio Tinto*, *Arch Coal (US)*, *BHPBilliton*, *Anglo American*, *Siberian Coal Energy (Russia)* and *Xstrata*.

Iron More than two-thirds of all global iron ore comes from just three companies: Brazil's *Compania Vale do Rio Doce (CVRD/Inco)*, *BHPBilliton* and *Rio Tinto*.

Gold *Barrick Gold (Barrick/Placer)* is the world's number-one gold miner, then *Newmont Mining, AngloGoldAshanti (Anglo American), Gold Fields of South Africa, Freeport McMoran (USA), Harmony Gold (South Africa), Navoi Metal and Mining (Uzbekistan), Compania de Minas Buenaventura SAA* and *Rio Tinto* (GFMS Ltd, *Gold Survey 2006*).

Diamonds By volume *Rio Tinto* is the global leader. By value *De Beers* is the biggest profiteer (with more than 70 per cent of the market) followed by *Alrosa* (Russia) and *Rio Tinto*.

Nickel The world's biggest producer is *Norilsk* of Russia, then *CVRD/Inco, Xstrata/Falconbridge* and *BHPBilliton*.

Notes

1 R. Moody, *Plunder: Presented by a Global Network of People Opposed to the Activities of the RTZ Corporation*, People Against RTZ and Its Subsidiaries (Partizans) and Campaign Against Foreign Control of Aoetearoa/New Zealand, London and Christchurch (NZ), 1991.

2 R. Moody, 'What has Bougainville to teach us?', Mines and Communities Website, September 2001.

3 'Bougainville mining courtship starts', *Post Courier*, Papua New Guinea, 18 August 2006.

4 See 'Brazilians invade company town of iron ore mine CVRD', Associated Press, 18 October 2006.

5 'Environment Canada flings door wide open to toxic waste dumping in Canada's lakes', Press release, MiningWatch Canada, 24 October 2006.

6 'Construction halted at part of Inco project: French judges find for indigenous group at troubled New Caledonia mine', *Toronto Globe and Mail*, 28 November 2006.

7 'Finished Business – Jabiluka goes to ground', *Sydney Morning Herald*, 29 April 2006.

8 'Rio Tinto's latest fall from grace', *London Calling*, Nostromo Research, London, 28 October 2006.

9 Obviously, mineral demand runs in cycles. During periods of major conflict, demand for ferrous and non-ferrous metals and strategic minerals booms; during times of economic depression, it will slump.

10 On mining the Arctic see D. Howden and B. Holst, 'Race for the Arctic', *Independent*, London, 5 January 2005; on mining the moon, see Interfax News Service, Russia, 5 January 2005; on deep sea mining, see *Mining Journal*, London, 27 February 2006 and 'Riches are calling from deep under the ocean', *Toronto Globe and Mail*, 24 May 2006.

11 Scientists at the Massachusetts Institute of Technology in 2006 claimed they had developed an electrolytic process to deliver 'carbon free' iron, whose rates of productivity could reach ten times that of aluminium. See 'New MIT technique eliminates greenhouse gases for iron production', Press statement, MIT, Boston, MA, 13 September 2006.

12 *Mining Journal*, London, 29 September 2006.

13 'Human Rights Council adopts text for indigenous rights', Press statement, United Nations Human Rights Council, 6 July 2006.

2 | How the World Bank backs bad miners

In 2001 the World Bank launched its Extractive Industries Review (EIR) to determine whether mining, oil and gas investment squared with its cardinal objective to abolish (or at least significantly reduce) global poverty. The review concluded that, generally speaking, it did not. But, soon after the EIR report was published in 2003, the bank rejected most of its recommendations. At a stroke the world's largest development agency thereby set aside the opinions of numerous analysts (including some of its own), hundreds of community and non-governmental organizations and that of Dr Emil Salim, the 'eminent person' entrusted with overseeing the review itself.

Salim is a former Indonesian minister for the environment, and was chair of all four preparatory committees for the 2002 Johannesburg World Summit for Sustainable Development (WSSD). Initially he had broadly supported the bank's funding of extractive industries and was sceptical about significantly reducing it. Many critics of mining feared he would pay scant attention to their experiences and some of them refused to participate in the EIR.

But, by the time he had taken evidence from civil society groups in central and eastern Europe, Africa and the Asia-Pacific region, and vital testimony from some indigenous communities, Salim had performed a U-turn. Presented in its draft form in 2003, his review called on the bank to phase out commitments to oil and gas over the next four years, and immediately withdraw support for the exploitation of coal. The bank must, said Salim, address the injustices, inequities and liabilities typified by other types of mining and redirect its resources to making good the damage its investments had already caused.[1] The bank should back projects only if they benefited local communities – especially vulnerable ethnic minorities, women and the poorest – assuring them '[a]n equitable share of the revenues'. Core International Labour Organization (ILO) standards must be followed and practical support given to workers laid off after mine closures. Ecologically critical habitats should be classified as 'no go areas', and urgent priority be given to promoting sources of renewable energy. Salim also unequivocally rejected the dumping of mine wastes into rivers and on to the seabed (Submarine Tailings Disposal or STD): these practices had already blighted his native land and, he said, clearly breached the 'precautionary principle'. But, perhaps most important, he demanded that indigenous peoples be granted the right to 'fully informed prior consent' (FIPC) to any extractive project before it be allowed to proceed.[2]

The bank's then president, James Wolfensohn, bridled at these demands. His management's response was to declare them 'not consistent with the World Bank Group mission of helping to fight poverty and improve the living standards of the people in the developing world'.[3] Although 'recognising' the legitimacy of benefit-sharing, the bank refused to commit to the guaranteed redistribution of corporate profits. It merely promised to 'help ensure that affected groups are not harmed by developments and, *where possible* [my emphasis], are better off'. The EIR's crucial insistence that mining-affected communities be entitled to exercise fully informed prior consent was rejected by the bank in favour of a 'commitment' to 'consultation' aimed at 'broad acceptance of the project by the affected community'. This, it claimed, would result in 'informed participation', thereby granting communities the opportunity to 'understand projects that will affect them'.

Wolfensohn's intransigence, and that of his directors, was greeted with anger and dismay by a raft of civil society groups

17

and prominent individuals. Cooperaccion, a leading Peruvian NGO working with miners and indigenous peoples, pointed out that '[t]he resettlement of communities to make way for extractive industry projects is intimately connected to the issue of consent ... The Bank's failure to unequivocally ban involuntary resettlement, a practice that *de facto* violates the economic, social and cultural rights of communities, reveals its unwillingness to make substantive change in the governance of extractive industry projects.'

In an exceptionally strident opinion, Nadia Martinez, of the US-based Institute for Policy Studies (IPS), condemned the bank for failing 'to distinguish its goals and standards from the likes of Halliburton, ExxonMobil, Shell, and other profit-driven institutions. US taxpayers' contributions to the World Bank are supposed to constitute international development assistance, not corporate handouts.' According to IPS research, 82 per cent of oil projects in which the bank has invested since 1992 ' ... are primarily designed for export of oil to the United States and Europe, Canada, Australia and Aoteaora/New Zealand and Japan'.[4]

Just as the bank dismissed the final version of the EIR, a leaked internal World Bank/International Finance Corporation (IFC) report confirmed Martinez's accusation. During the first nine months of its 2004 financial year (FY 2004) just half a dozen oil, gas and mining investments accounted for no less than 56 per cent of all dividend and related returns to the IFC. The extractive sector was exposed as a money-spinner the bank could ill afford to snub, let alone forsake. In October that year, the director of the World Bank's Oil, Gas and Chemicals Department, Rashad Kaldany, spoke of a 'new climate of optimism as global metal prices reach record levels'. The bank would, he declared, increase its investments in mining so long as companies came up with environmental safeguards and 'more transparent book keeping'.[5] For financial year 2005, IFC's investments in oil, gas and mining, along with those devoted to primary and non-metallic metals production, were just under a fifth of its total US$8.3 billion portfolio.[6]

At first glance the amount of equity (shares) directly held in mining companies, and of debt finance provided to the minerals industry, may make the IFC seem 'a relatively small player from a global perspective'. From 1993 to 2001 it financed thirty-three mining projects to the tune of US$681 million, around 18 per cent of the total project costs. Annually, out of around US$30 billion invested in mining worldwide, less than 2 per cent has historically come from the IFC.[7]

But simple statistics undervalue the bank's critical, twenty-two-year-old role in 'reforming' rules of entry to mineral-endowed states in the South on behalf of hundreds of external private minerals companies and investors. The bank's structural adjustment programmes (SAPs) have driven nations like Guyana, Peru and Zambia into high-risk privatization processes or over-dependency on mineral extraction. A significant number of damaging mines would never have been constructed had it not been for IFC investment or political risk insurance cover provided by MIGA, the IFC's Multilaterial Investment Guarantee Agency.[8] Equally important, World Bank 'standards' and 'guidelines' have become the performance benchmarks purportedly followed by private banks, multilateral institutions, some insurers and export credit agencies: notably the Organization for Economic Cooperation and Development (OECD) and the forty investment banks signed up to the so-called Equator Principles. Yet, for the past six years, these key principles have many times been betrayed by the bank itself.

Code-breaking

The bank has a long history of engagement with the minerals industry. Between 1955 and 1990 mining-related public sector grants were mainly channelled through the International

Bank for Reconstruction and Development (IBRD) and the International Development Association (IDA) into five main areas: 'reform and rehabilitation' (in Guyana, Bolivia and Ghana); 'greenfield' mine construction (as in China and Jordan); mineral processing (for example, Jamaican bauxite-alumina); technical assistance (as provided to Gecamines in the former Zaire); and engineering work. Over these thirty-five years, nearly fifty mining or mineral processing projects were supported with loans and credits totalling just under US$2 billion. Undoubtedly the most widely criticized of all at this time was Ferro Carajas, initiated in 1981. This huge iron ore mine lay at the centre of Brazil's Grande Carajas resource colonization programme, which was ultimately to cover more than 10 per cent of the country's land mass and 16 per cent of Amazonia itself.[9]

During this period the bank introduced its first batch of revised mineral codes, aimed at attracting increased foreign investment to mineral-dependent economies and encouraging them to at least start privatizing their mining companies. Meanwhile, thirty-five sub-Saharan African governments were being forced by the World Bank and the International Monetary Fund (IMF) to implement 162 structural adjustment programmes (more than all other SAPs imposed at the time elsewhere in the world). In 1988 the bank's Mining Unit invited forty-five major mining companies (with combined mineral sales of US$40 billion) to prescribe how Southern states ought to behave towards the private sector in future. The companies urged 'the reduction of personnel, and even mine closure in response to economic reasons [*sic*] and to regulate the right of strike in order to avoid unnecessary conflicts where confrontations could be avoided'. The companies placed 'greatest importance' on the bank 'work[ing] with individual countries to update and reform existing mining investment codes'.[10] Another set of codes was launched the following year, aimed at more African states, eastern and central Europe,

Latin America and the Asia-Pacific region. In some instances these codes were to undermine regulations dating back several decades (in Venezuela to 1945, and in India to 1947), originally aimed at retaining wealth within the country and preventing foreign takeovers.

Until 1992 state-owned mining companies had largely been left intact. That year the bank published *The Strategy for African Mining*, marking a policy sea change – and not just for Africa. This argued that public ownership of mining enterprises was a hindrance to attracting foreign direct investment and that many such companies had meanwhile become ineffectual and corrupt. From now on these laggards ought to adhere to 'market discipline' in order to reduce risks to private capital – and this meant not just being taken out of public hands but, in some cases, dismantled as well. New projects would aim primarily at production for export rather than value-adding at home. Funding for exploration and development should be redirected to 'qualified firms' – almost exclusively from North America, Europe, Australia and Japan. Investment legislation, foreign exchange regulations, taxation and labour laws in poorer, mining-dependent countries would all be further 'streamlined'. The bank would 'improve' the former mining codes 'where issues refer to the access by the investors to mining rights, the politics [*sic*] with respect to mining rights, and the role and scope of the state owned enterprises'.[11] Not only was freer and cheaper access being offered to mineral deposits, but the keys to the 'deposit box' itself.

Within five years, the negative impacts of this second set of 'reforms' were reverberating in a large number of countries, especially Peru, Brazil, India and the Philippines. In April 1997 Brazilians took to the streets in protest at the government's planned privatization of Companhia Vale do Rio Doce (CVRD), Latin America's biggest state-owned mining company and the world's premier iron ore miner, thanks to its Grande Carajas exploits. The dissidents feared losing hard-earned pension funds and that their economic power would be concentrated even further in the hands of 'oligopolistic' institutions. Critics of the sale included former presidents Jose Sarney and Itamar Franco, and the Workers' Party senator Ms Benedeta da Silva, who called it 'a theft against the Brazilian people'. Meanwhile, more than a hundred injunctions, seeking to block denationalization, piled up in the courts to no avail.

The Philippines 1995 Mining Act not only broke the country's hallowed 60/40 rule (guaranteeing majority Filipino ownership of domestic enterprises), but also allowed overseas companies to lease huge expanses of new territory, securing extraction rights for twenty-five years or more. After nationwide protests by scores of non-governmental organizations the country's Supreme Court ruled in February 2004 that a full foreign takeover of minerals was 'unconstitutional'; at which point pro-mining forces within the Arroyo government allegedly pressured the court to ensure that the decision would be overturned.

These and other public outcries against new mineral policies pushed the World Bank – if reluctantly – towards a minor rethink. Following the publication in 1997 of the policy document *Assistance for Minerals Sector Development and Reform in Member Countries*[12] a third set of codes was promulgated, purporting to pay attention to the views of project-affected peoples, and insisting on mandatory environmental impact assessments. Today these updated codes continue being incorporated into new mineral legislation for South-based economies, applied in particular to 'post-conflict' African states and Central Asia. Although they may differ in detail from country to country, the new rules generally allow tax holidays of up to ten years; the abolition of customs duties on imports of equipment; reduced withholding taxes and income tax rates (usually 30 per cent or lower); tax relief for operating losses and mine closure costs; relief for any charges on prospecting rights; and up to a 100 per cent repatriation of profits.

And so the resistance continues. Efforts by Colombian trade unionists to prevent a sell-off of the state mining enterprise Minercol in 2003/04 triggered death threats against their leaders, who had accused lawyers, acting for overseas companies (notably cement companies Cemex and Holcim), of framing the legislation at the behest of the World Bank. Some governments have also – if belatedly – tried to claw back what they lost over the previous two decades of neoliberalization. In 2004 the Peruvian government announced a sliding 1–3 per cent royalty on gross mineral sales. Despite the modesty of the proposal, multinational mining companies, led by Barrick Gold of Canada, vigorously protested, threatening to withdraw from the country. On the election of neoliberal president Alan Garcia in mid-2006, the industry was mollified when he invited the mining companies to make 'voluntary' payments and thus escape the imposition of royalties or a windfall profits tax.[13] The same year, the presidents of Venezuela and Bolivia both undertook to renationalize their countries' minerals industry (a project in considerable doubt at the time of writing – see Chapter 3). Mongolia had reluctantly passed a Mining Act in 2005, opening its doors so favourably to foreign investment that some fifty gold companies were clambering over the territory within the year. But, after a major cabinet reshuffle, in mid-2006 the government asserted its right to take up to a 34 per cent interest in all mine projects.

Broken promises

For years, the bank's avowed intention has been to rescue 'failed states' blighted by corruption, nepotism, over-employment, mismanagement and high grading (the exploitation of richer ores for profit in the short term, while abandoning lower-grade, but recoverable, reserves). These factors, claimed the bank, had resulted in indebtedness and impoverishment. By gearing to competitive markets, bloated and subsidized workforces would be cut back; commodity output tailored to global demand; safer technologies introduced by the private sector; and sustainable incomes generated for all.[14] In reality, none of these promises has been fulfilled. There is little evidence that corruption has significantly diminished: in Peru, for example, the US company Newmont paid bribes to secure its huge Yanacocha concession.[15] The practice of 'high grading' may have diminished but this is largely in response to a rising demand which has made the working of lower-grade ores more economic. Above all, the dismemberment of state-owned enterprises has not improved living standards, resulted in increased employment (see Chapter 5) or 'captured' for the national economy anything like the projected returns.

Few objective analyses have so far been published on the overall impacts of the bank's revisionary mining codes. One of them is a 2003 study by the Groupe de recherche sur les activités minières' (GRAMA), based at the University of Quebec in Montreal. This cites Ghana's experience as most indicative of the retrograde changes; all the more relevant given the state's relatively fair record of combating corruption and its status as one of the most important recipients of gold-related investment over the last decade. Yes, agrees GRAMA, the new legislation has stimulated a 'mining boom'. Nevertheless, the sector possesses a limited capacity to generate additional local employment. Meanwhile, at least 71 per cent of the country's mineral value had been siphoned into foreign-held accounts. From 1992 until 2003, minerals represented around 40 per cent of Ghana's total merchandise export earnings. But less than 3 per cent of these earnings actually contributed to the nation's gross domestic product. The new mining regulations were 'characterized by such an absence of regulatory mechanisms that the situation came to be recognized as largely detrimental to the mining industry itself'. The term 'good governance', so cherished by the bank, had been primarily interpreted within the country as 'creating a favourable environment for investment ... [D]evelopment objectives ... were given little emphasis'.[16]

Furthermore, said GRAMA, in some other countries (such as Guinea) the state's former role as protector of social and environmental rights had been severely weakened at precisely the point it should have been strengthened. Over a decade's concentration on attracting inward private investment had left government bodies with precious little structural capacity to enforce any improvements. Together, the bank and the mining industry had ruthlessly driven down the costs of exploiting South-based mineral deposits; very little was returning to the exchequer for 'development', while profits continued to flow offshore.[17] The point was borne out by Canadian minerals researcher Bonnie Campbell: 'In the absence of a central power which holds internal and local political legitimacy, the process of privatisation in favour of foreign companies may affect not only certain functions of the state but entire regions of the country.' It could be argued, says Campbell, that 'state-owned mining interests are more likely [than private ones] to embrace the long term management of regional, amorphous, environmental degradation'.[18]

One heavy irony is that, far from failing, some disposed-of state companies were actually making healthy profits at the time of privatization. This was the case with Balco, India's third-largest aluminium company, which was 'disinvested' in 2001 to Sterlite Industries (now Vedanta Resources plc) at what some critics claimed was only a tenth of its true asset value.[19] The same was true of Brazil's CVRD, prompting one commentator, Flavio E. N. Hegenberg, to declare: 'In practice privatisation has been used more to highlight the commitment to market oriented reforms than to redeem debt or increase efficiency.'[20]

Box 2.1 Unconsolidating copper

Zambia boasts the richest copper deposits on the African continent. In 2000, the IFC embarked on asset-stripping the legendary state-owned enterprise Zambia Consolidated Copper Mines. A new company, Konkola Copper Mines plc (KCM), emerged from the wreckage, with its major shareholding in the hands of Anglo American Corporation (AAC), and smaller equities owned by the British Commonwealth Development Corporation (CDC) Capital Partners and the Zambian government. Within eighteen months, however, KCM was on the brink of dissolution, unable to meet production targets and to reduce costs in the teeth of a deteriorating market.[21] Much to the bank's alarm, Anglo American then ditched the enterprise, leaving the Zambian government to pull together another corporate 'rescue' supported by the World Bank/IFC and CDC. In mid-2004 Vedanta Resources plc, a London-listed company 54 per cent owned by Indian mine financier Anil Agarwal, finally secured KCM from the Zambian government for under US$50 million, but with no guaranteed capital to improve workers' wages and construct safer plant. This cut-price deal revived concerns, originally expressed by researcher Patricia Feeney in 2001, that workers' health, safety and rights to compensation, as well as urgently required environmental improvements at the mine, would be sacrificed to expediency.[22] In 2005, with copper prices booming, Vedanta set about a large-scale expansion, opening up an underground deposit and constructing a new state-of-the-art smelter. The profits were undoubtedly rolling into the UK company but, as revealed in mid-2006, the government's share of distributable income from KCM had not substantially improved over the previous two years.[23]

Sustained non-development

In January 1999, Peter van der Veen, the World Bank's head of mining, expressed confidence that, though states had largely ceased being 'owner/operators' of mining assets, they had none the less become 'regulator/administrators' operating alongside the companies. Now, affirmed van der Veen, governments could 'increasingly negotiate with indigenous peoples, local communities, and NGOs, any of which can influence, even stop, the development of a mining project'. Added van der Veen: 'The old enclave model for development is rarely going to be considered a viable alternative for large mining projects.'[24] The Business Partners for Development (BPD) initiative, launched by the bank the previous year, was intended to demonstrate that governments, businesses and civil society could indeed work together, brokering projects of benefit to them all in so-called 'tri-sectoral' partnerships. The natural resources component ('cluster') of the BPD saw the bank lined up with the UK Department for International Development (DfID) and the development charity CARE to provide support for seven extractive projects. The initiative – at least the extractives initiative – was an almost unmitigated disaster, however. One of the cases, the Utkal aluminium joint venture in India, had to be hastily withdrawn from the programme after three non-violent local villagers were shot dead by police just prior to a planned field visit by the bank. The Transredes Bolivia–Brazil pipeline project was substituted. But this also foundered following a citizens' uprising against the scheme in 2003, which contributed directly to the downfall and abdication of Bolivian president 'Goni' Lozado. In the final analysis, the BPD could present only two remotely good examples of the partnership concept. Even so, the IFC withdrew from one of these in 2002 – the Sarshatali coal mine in India – on discovering that bank guidelines had not been followed by the private company in charge.[25]

The naive optimism expressed by van der Veen in 1999

was further undermined in 2003 by a consultant within the World Bank's own Operations Evaluation Department (OED). M. A. Thomas had been asked to determine how far the bank had been 'factoring governance' into its extractive industries 'approach' to Chile, Ecuador, Ghana, Kazakhstan, Papua New Guinea and Tanzania, between 1993 and 2002. 'Paradoxically,' concluded Thomas, 'although a few countries have bootstrapped themselves to higher incomes through the judicious exploitation of such resources, an abundance of natural resources is more often associated with poor economic performance ... Most EI [Extractive Industry] projects are not the result of a governance-informed sector assistance strategy.' Even the mining projects that did pursue such a strategy showed 'no indication that the decision to support increased investment was preceded by an analysis that considered the likely benefits and risks of such investment in light of the quality of governance'.[26] Historically, said Thomas, 'the Bank's approach to the EI sector appears to treat increased private investment as the primary goal and a good in itself'.[27] In reality, 'increased EI investment is likely to lead to bad development outcomes for many if not most of the Bank's clients'.[28] In the worst case, the EI sector can bring little public benefit and can leave long-term costs behind in the form of environmental destruction and war.[29] Local communities 'bear the brunt of accompanying environmental damage, health risks, property takings and damage, and changes to traditional life and culture'.[30] Thomas concluded that the bank 'risks facilitating the wastage of the country's non-renewable resources, as well as contributing to environmental damage, violence, and weakening of the quality of governance itself'.[31]

Bad marks all round

Not deterred by mounting criticisms, the bank clings to the claim that investment in large-scale extractive industry can turn around a company's bad environmental and human rights performance, compelling it to raise its game. This is perhaps the greatest single fallacy, as can be demonstrated by many failed enterprises up to the present.

Guyana 1995–96 In one critical case, the IFC 'rolled over' its financing, despite a massive previous failure. Following a spectacular breach of Guyana's Omai mine tailings (wastes) dam in August 1995 the IFC's political risk insurance agency, the Multilateral Investment Guarantee Agency (MIGA), renewed its insurance cover instead of cancelling it. The dam collapse resulted in some 4 billion cubic litres of cyanide and other heavy metals cascading into a local creek, then into the country's main waterway, the Essequibo river. MIGA, together with Canada's Export Development Corporation, had provided political risk insurance cover (worth US$49.8 million) for the mine's Canadian partners, Cambior and Golden Star Resources. But the agency failed to adequately scrutinize the mine's standards of construction or monitor its operation. MIGA stood by as the tailings dam wall was raised far above limits set in the original Environmental Impact Assessment. The government and companies rushed the mine into a reopening in 1996, albeit with several technical improvements, but before a parliamentary sub-commission on the disaster had delivered its final conclusions. Having promoted Omai as a prime example of large-scale minerals-related investment critical to a highly indebted Third World state, the bank was hardly going to argue against its reopening. According to a Guyana member of parliament, MIGA told the Omai sub-commission, set up to investigate the disaster, that, if the government imposed any new environmental regulations on the mine, it would be 'tantamount to nationalisation', compelling MIGA to pay compensation to Cambior and Golden Star.[32]

Papua New Guinea and West Papua 1995–96 The IFC has also ignored strictures, made by a fellow investment guarantee agency, against supporting two major mine projects in the Pacific. In 1995, the US government's Overseas Private Investment Corporation (OPIC) – the world's second-largest export credit agency – refused to underwrite the Lihir gold project in Papua New Guinea, because Rio Tinto intended employing Submarine Tailings Disposal (STD) in violation of at least one international treaty to which the USA was a signatory.[33] Among the instruments cited by OPIC in support of this decision were the London Convention on Dumping at Sea, the US Clean Water Act and the Marine Protection Research and Sanctuaries Act.[34]

The following year OPIC also accused Freeport-Rio Tinto of violating its PRI cover for the vast Grasberg copper-gold mine in West Papua by doubling production rates and thus enormously increasing the burden of contaminating wastes ejected into the Ajkwa river system. The companies angrily rejected the accusation and OPIC removed its insurance cover, but MIGA refused to do so.

Russia 2000–01 More than seventy Russian and international NGOs called on the bank in 2000 not to support environmentally sensitive projects – including mining operations – following abolition by Vladimir Putin, the country's new president, of Russia's main environmental agency. Despite this, MIGA granted US\$27.2 million of political risk cover to Canada's Bema Gold for construction of the Julietta gold and silver mine in Magadan province. No information on the project or its social and environmental impacts was released by MIGA before issuing the guarantee. A technical expert found in early 2001 that Bema had already violated good practice principles. The tailings dam was precariously located on land that was 'far larger than needed … stripped down to the permafrost level [with] the insulating and moisture-absorbing layers of soil, tundra and organic material removed'. The dam was 'less than 50 yards from a stream and two kilometres from a major river which could be affected by seepage or a larger cyanide spill'. Friends of the Earth International took up these issues in *Risky Business*, its 2001 critique of MIGA's policy and performance.[35]

MIGA brusquely denied the allegations, without offering any supporting evidence. Retorted FOE:

> MIGA seems to be content that no disaster has yet happened, rather than attempt to find out whether the project design has the potential to lead to a major disaster and to avert this possibility ... We have found MIGA to be unduly resistant to reform ... This has led many organisations to conclude that MIGA has little interest in conforming its policies and practices with the World Bank's mission of poverty alleviation, and ... to conclude that MIGA should therefore no longer function as part of the World Bank Group.[36]

Zaire/DRC 1997–2002 As bloody conflicts over resource control raged in Zaire during the nineties, American Mineral Fields became the chief vehicle used by its founder and major shareholder, Jean-Raymond Boulle, to expand into Africa and create a personal fiefdom, specifically in Zaire (now the Democratic Republic of Congo or DRC). Boulle has been described as 'a powerful private player with access to significant amounts of money, raw materials, military technology and even a private rapid reaction force, [who] can deviously pursue his own private agenda. That is what Boulle does.'[37]

Boulle gained the lucrative Kolwezi mineral workings in 1997 as a reward for lending then rebel leader Kabila his private jet and donating US$1 billion to Kabila's campaign against the dictator Mobutu. Later, AMF was accused of links to two London-based paramilitary forces: International Defence and Security

(IDS), a spin-off from the notorious Executive Outcomes (EO) mercenary force, and British-based Defence Systems Ltd, also active in appropriating mineral resources from conflict areas.[38] Just before the IFC backed Boulle's Kolwezi project, AMF was condemned by a UN panel of experts investigating companies operating in the Democratic Republic of Congo, for violations of the OECD Guidelines for Multinational Enterprises. Yet these rules are themselves invoked by the bank as a basis of its own human rights guidelines.

Sierra Leone 1991–2002 In 2001 the IFC resumed funding for Sierra Rutile Ltd (SRL)'s ilmenite mine in Sierra Rutile, following its closure when besieged by forces of the murderous Revolutionary United Front (RUF) between 1994 and 1995. The loan was cancelled in late 2002 because SRL found alternative finance. The first tranche of IFC funding was agreed in 1991, three years after the mine came on-stream, and backed by Britain's Commonwealth Development Corporation (CDC) in order to expand SRL's production from 150,000 to 200,000 tonnes a year. This was despite the fact that OREINT, an environmental rights NGO based in the capital Freetown, had already damned SRL's performance, claiming that no adequate Environmental Impact Assessments were carried out before the loans were agreed. OREINT's report *Mined Out* was circulated in draft in 1994 and published (revised) under the auspices of Friends of the Earth UK in 1997.[39] It detailed land degradation, flooding and pollution, with associated risks to health caused by the wet dredging methods used by SRL, alongside the 'complete relocation of villages and their inhabitants, often against their wishes'.[40] In 1992 a tailings dam constructed by SRL collapsed, destroying ten villages and leaving 10,000 people homeless, as well as intensifying waterborne diseases, such as malaria, cholera and polio.

By 1997, 5,300 villagers had been forced to move. Representatives of the company themselves acknowledged that 'some villages were resettled in places where ... water and farmland were grossly inadequate and where the general sanitation ... was critical'. In addition, villagers complained that (under a community resettlement and health programme managed by CARE) they were dumped on inadequate and inferior land, resulting in the depletion of freshwater fish and bush meat. Restoration of mined-out land, in the absence of topsoil, was severely limited, while 'damage to the original ecosystem will probably be irreversible'.[41]

After five years of conflict, in 1996 SRL approached the IFC for further finance to repair war damage and complete the mine's expansion. The bank commissioned a more comprehensive EIA which none the less failed to address the critical issues in the OREINT-FOE report. It also ignored SRL's continued employment of the services of the brutal South African mercenary force EO, originally employed by the company to recapture its mine from RUF marauders in November 1995.

Peru 1993–2006 The Yanacocha gold mine, operated by Newmont of the USA in Peru's Cajamarca province, is Latin America's premier gold producer and promoted by the IFC as its minerals flagship on the subcontinent. In practice the World Bank has demonstrated a woeful lack of project oversight, failure to evaluate the project's liabilities and contempt for local indigenous peoples' rights. The mine's 'development' outcome is one that even bank consultants have acknowledged to be defective.

The enterprise had already been opposed by Cajamarca's indigenous communities long before its first gold was poured in 1993. Opposition mounted between May that year and June 1999, when IFC funding and undertakings reached US$151.7 million. In fact, the IFC did not regard either the mine or its host country as risk free. On the contrary, its investment was specifically aimed at providing 'political comfort' (*sic*) to Newmont and its domestic partner, in the face of marked investor reluctance to back Peruvian mining.

In June 2000, shortly after the IFC made its heaviest invest-ment in the project, 151 kilos of mercury spilled from a truck leav-ing the Yanacocha site, causing eight people to be hospitalized.[42] Some thousand residents, along with the municipal authorities, filed lawsuits against Newmont in its home state of Colorado, alleging injury as a result of the disaster. The company was also fined half a million US dollars by Peru's Mining and Energy Ministry. Meg Taylor, the bank's newly appointed Compliance Advisory Officer, acknowledged that the company had failed to avert the disaster – startlingly adding that the Peruvian govern-ment had 'no relevant ... regulations regarding the transportation of mercury or other hazardous materials [*sic*]'.[43]

While the IFC continued asserting that Yanacocha promoted large-scale employment, two bank personnel threw strong doubt on some of its other claims. Consultants Gary McMahon and Felix Remy pointed out in late 2001 that, though 'substantial taxes from a mining operation ... should go to the local and regional levels', it was 'unclear if they actually have'.[44] Examining rises in mining-associated prostitution, 'related diseases' and alcohol abuse at six major mines, McMahon and Remy found that these problems were 'most evident in Cajamarca'.[45]

With claims for compensation related to the 2000 disaster still not settled, in February 2006 farmers successfully stopped Newmont from opening a new mine site at Cerro Quilish, also in Cajamarca. Just seven months later, another campesino com-munity brought the company's explorations to a halt at the Cara-chugo prospect, claiming it had contaminated water supplies. Although an eleven-point agreement was signed in September 2006, promising improved water monitoring and quality, com-munity leader Marco Arana announced that: 'The conflict has not ended, and will never end if the problem continues to be dealt with in a superficial manner.'

Wolfowitz in sheep's clothing

When Paul Wolfowitz took over the reins of the World Bank as president in 2005, his hawkish past led many civil society organizations to fear he would strip out even the less contentious planks of bank policy, while adding rotten ones of his own. To date he has not done so: his recent proposal to strengthen 'conditionalities' has divided 'bank watchers' into those who want more, not less, autonomy provided to client states on how they spend grants and loans; and those who welcome them as a further tool to limit corruption. The EIR has not been totally discarded: a bank assessment of its supposed implementation was published in December 2005, to be met with a critical rejoinder from the Central and Eastern European Bankwatch Network.[46]

Policy and performance standards aimed at 'social and environmental sustainability' have, to a limited extent, been revised upwards. With great fanfare the bank has launched its clean and renewable energy programmes and, in China at least, backed them with substantial funding.

Certainly the IFC's proposed standards of February 2006 include provisions with which few would argue: comprehensive social assessment for all proposed private sector loans; client compliance with ILO and UN labour principles; the annual public release of client implementation reports. The 'improvement' of living standards for displaced persons remains, however, merely a 'policy objective'. There is no commitment to uphold international law, including human rights protocols, or to screen prospective clients for their past record, and no insistence on providing equivalent-quality 'land for land' for those displaced from their homes, forests, fields and rivers. Above all, the bank's rubric addressing the rights of indigenous peoples is rife with vague and ambiguous language.

The cardinal demand of the EIR was for Free Prior Informed community Consent (FPIC). The bank continues to reject this precept in favour of nugatory 'consultation'.[47] The IFC promises to carry out its own 'investigations' on whether a project has earned 'broad community support', but this is not incorporated into its performance standards; instead it remains a mere policy 'objective'. While one new safeguard is supposed to establish a 'successful outcome' to negotiations at the community level, it is not at all clear what this means in practice. Some community members will boycott such negotiations on principle; others may have been inveigled into them through bribes or the promise of jobs. Many will simply not understand what they are being asked to sign up to. No binding social contracts or guarantees of profit sharing are envisaged between a private operator and project-affected peoples – only that the client should 'identify' development 'opportunities'.[48]

The bank's own in-house study of September 2005, *Where is the Wealth of Nations?*, challenged the use of conventional national accounting figures – specifically GNP (gross national product) – as a valid means of assessing human development standards. In a statement launching the report, the bank itself admitted that improved accounting of the real value of natural resources and their accelerating depletion, combined with population growth, 'shows that net savings per person are negative in the world's most impoverished countries, particularly in sub-Saharan Africa'. According to the report, 'natural capital', including minerals as well as forests, pastureland and protected areas, had to date been grossly undervalued. Preserving these resources would now be essential to reducing poverty, especially in sub-Saharan Africa – precisely where the bank's structural adjustment programmes had hit hardest. Yet the bank still refuses to back its own horse;

nothing has shaken its confidence in mining as a key engine to promote sustainable development. On the contrary, during the two years since Wolfowitz came to power, the IFC has thrown its money at further bad projects, ignoring their likely environmental impacts, the provenance and record of the companies behind them and, above all, the strident opposition of local communities and NGOs.

Democratic Republic of Congo 2005–06 In late 2005, a coalition of Congolese and international NGOs wrote to bank president Wolfowitz declaring Anvil Mining's Dikulushi copper-silver mine to be symbolic of the bank's failure to 'uphold its commitments to protect the rights of people affected by extractive industry projects'. This was the first mine in the DRC to get World Bank support and was touted as contributing to post-conflict recovery and as a catalyst for further private sector mineral investments.

IFC/MIGA had issued a US$13.3 political risk guarantee for the second-stage expansion of the mine in May the previous year, saying there were no serious security risks. Nevertheless, since June 2004 NGOs have accused MIGA of failing to ensure Anvil's compliance with voluntary principles on the use of security forces, and the UN norms for transnational corporations.

In October 2004 trucks loaned by Anvil to the Congolese army (FARDC) were used to transport troops to Kilwa, approximately 50 kilometres south of the mine, where they slaughtered fifty unarmed members of a rebel group. The bank's Compliance Advisor Ombudsman (CAO) later carried out an audit of MIGA's due diligence on the project, which was withheld by the bank from publication for several months. When it was finally released in early 2006, the CAO confirmed that the company had indeed materially assisted the military in carrying out the atrocity and that MIGA should have been aware of this strong possibility.

Nevertheless, the political risk insurance cover was not withdrawn.

The United Nations unit, MONUC, carried out a detailed investigation into this atrocity, which revealed links between Anvil Mining and the DRC government, as well as the company's failure to follow the guidelines on collaborating with military forces.[49]

Guatemala 2004–06 Against strident community opposition, in June 2004 the IFC approved a $45 million loan to Canadian Glamis Gold's Marlin mine project in Guatemala's predominantly indigenous western highlands region. The following January, a forty-day protest by local villagers, concerned at the mine's potential environmental impacts, ended in bloodshed as security forces clashed with protesters, resulting in one death and dozens of injuries.

On 13 March 2005, a villager was shot dead by an off-duty employee of Grupo Golan, a company providing 'security' for Glamis. Two months later, a report issued by the Guatemalan Human Rights Ombudsman argued that the licence for the Glamis mine should be revoked because of the government's violation of International Labour Organization (ILO) Convention 169, on Indigenous and Tribal Peoples, which affords indigenous peoples the right to prior consultation regarding the use of natural resources on and under their lands. In June, the rural municipality bordering the mine site held a referendum on the project in which 98 per cent of the more than two thousand participants voted against the project. Meanwhile the World Bank's CAO had carried out an investigation into allegations by Madre Selva, a Guatemalan environmental organization, that the IFC (*inter alia*) violated the requirement of prior consultation with indigenous peoples and that the mines' existence exacerbated social tensions, violence and insecurity. The CAO agreed that there had not been adequate consultation, nor a thorough assessment of the mine's potential social and environmental impacts. The IFC had also failed to assess the Guatemalan government's capacity to effectively mitigate conflicts and regulate the project – a capacity that the CAO described as virtually non-existent. Faced with a regulatory void, the CAO found that Glamis was applying its own, improvised, protocols and developing its activities on an ad hoc basis.

In fact – although this was revealed only after the loan had been approved – the IFC's own board of directors had expressed unusually strong reservations about the project and sharply questioned its development benefits to Guatemala, noting that the $261 million project would create only 160 long-term jobs and pay royalties of just 1 per cent of its revenues. The board had also expressed concern that IFC was relying on information from the company, rather than an independent assessment, in order to refute concerns expressed by NGOs.[50]

Ghana 2006 At the end of January 2006, the bank approved a US$75 million IFC loan to Newmont Mining for its Ahafo gold project. An alliance of advocacy and environmental groups had urged a postponement until there were proper safeguards to protect the 9,000 people who, it said, would lose their land and livelihoods and face contamination of their drinking water from mine wastes. Rashad Kaldany, who heads the bank's oil, gas, mining and chemicals department, freely acknowledged that the company – then the world's biggest gold producer – could finance the project on its own. However, said Kaldany, it wanted 'the agency's stamp of approval for meeting social and environmental standards'.[51]

One of the undertakings given by Newmont was broken as soon as the mine came on-stream in mid-2006. Seventy-four villagers, protesting that the company had woefully broken its promise to recruit 50 per cent of the workforce from local residents, were attacked by security forces protecting the project.[52]

Notes

1 E. Salim, *The Extractive Industries Review: Final Report*, presented to the World Bank, Washington, DC, November 2003.

2 Ibid.

3 *Financial Times*, London, 3 February 2004.

4 N. Martinez, 'More evidence of how the World Bank teams up with profit, not the poor!', *New Internationalist*, Oxford, November 2004, p. 6.

5 'World Bank to boost investment in mining projects', *WB Press Review*, 12 October 2004.

6 World Bank/IFC Annual Report, summary, 2006.

7 Mining, Minerals and Sustainable Development project: final report, *Breaking New Ground*, Earthscan Publications, London and Sterling, VA, 2002, p. 135.

8 See R. Moody, *The Risks We Run: Mining, Communities and Political Risk Insurance*, International Books, Utrecht, 2005.

9 The consequences of constructing this project and its infrastructure are summarized in B. Rich, *Mortgaging the Earth: The World Bank, Environmental Impoverishment and the Crisis of Development*, Earthscan, London, 1994, pp. 26, 27, 29–33. See also B. Zagema, R. Moody, K. Blauw and R. Boon, *Taking Responsibility: Metal Mining, People and the Environment*, Friends of the Earth Netherlands (Milieudefensie), Amsterdam, 1997, pp. 16–18.

10 See F. Remy, *World Bank Financing for the Mining Sector*, Mining Unit, Industry and Energy Division, Africa Technical Dept, World Bank: Address to the International Lead and Zinc Study Group, São Paulo, 7 February 1991.

11 *The Strategy for African Mining*, World Bank Technical Paper no. 181, Washington, DC, 1992.

12 W. T. Onorato, P. Fox and J. Strongman, *World Bank Group Assistance for Minerals Sector Development and Reform in Member Countries*, Washington, DC, 18 December 1997.

13 Reuters, Lima, 24 August 2006.

14 K. Anderson, 'Mining, privatisation and the environment', *Raw Materials Report: Journal of Minerals Policy, Business and the Environment*, Stockholm, 11(3): 26.

15 J. Perlez and L. Bergman, 'The cost of gold – treasure of Yanacocha: tangled strands in fight over Peru gold mine', *New York Times*, 25 October 2005.

16 Groupe de recherche sur les activités minières (GRAMA), 'The challenge of development. Mining codes in Africa and corporate responsibility', in E. Bastide, T. Wade and J. Warden (eds), *International and Comparitive Mineral Law and Policy*, Centre for Energy, Petroleum

and Mineral Law and Policy, University of Dundee, 2003, summarized in *Mining Journal*, London, 14 February 2003, p. 106.

17 Ibid.

18 B. Campbell, 'Liberalisation, deregulation, state promoted investment – Canadian mining interests in Africa', *Raw Materials Report: Journal of Mineral Policy, Business and Environment*, Stockholm, 1998, 13(4): 16.

19 C. P. Chandrasekhar, 'Lessons from the Balco Fiasco', Macroscan Internet news service, 22 February 2001.

20 F. E. N. Hegenberg, 'Brazilian mining industry in the age of liberalisation', *Raw Materials Report*, 1997, 12(3): 8.

21 IFC Quarterly Report on IFC Project Activities, Washington, DC, June 2002, p. 26.

22 P. Feeney, *The Limitations of Corporate Social Responsibility on Zambia's Copperbelt: Konkola Copper Mines (KCM): Environmental Management Plan (May 2001)*, Oxfam, Oxford, 2001.

23 'Zambia: record copper prices, but mine region yet to benefit', IRIN, Lusaka, 28 June 2006.

24 P. van der Veen, 'The World Bank's role in mineral development', PricewaterhouseCooper paper delivered to the Global Mining Conference, San Francisco, CA, 1–3 June 1999.

25 R. Moody, *The Risks We Run: Mining, Communities and Political Risk Insurance*, International Books, Utrecht, 2005, pp. 86–8.

26 M. A. Thomas, *Evaluation of the World Bank Group's Activities in the Extractive Industries*, Background paper, OED-World Bank, Washington, DC, 2003, p. 11.

27 Ibid.

28 Ibid., p. 20.

29 Ibid., p. 3.

30 Ibid., p. 60.

31 Ibid., p. 13.

32 See 'Community leaders of riverain communities affected by the 1995 Omai cyanide spill', Letter to Gerald T. West, MIGA, 18 March 2000.

33 G. Evans, J. Goodman and N. Lansbury, *Moving Mountains: Communities Confront Mining and Globalisation*, Zed Books, London, 2002, pp. 46–7.

34 See R. Moody, *Into the Unknown Regions: The Hazards of STD*, International Books and Society of St Columban, Utrecht and London, 2001, p. 56.

35 Friends of the Earth International, *Risky Business*, Washington, DC, 2001.

36 Carol Welch and others, FOEI letter to MIGA, Washington, DC, April 2002.

37 J. Peleman, 'Mining for serious trouble: Jean-Raymond Boulle and his corporate empire project', in *Mercenaries: An African Security Dilemma*, Pluto Press, London, 2000, pp. 165–6. See also R. Moody, 'Out of Africa: mining in the Congo basin', in *The Congo Basin/Le bassin du Congo*, IUCN, Amsterdam, 1998, p. 137.

38 A.-F. Musah and J. K. Fayemi (eds), *Mercenaries: An African Security Dilemma*, Pluto Press, London, 2000, p. 69.

39 *Mined Out: The Environmental and Social Implications of Development Finance in Rutile Mining in Sierra Leone*, Friends of the Earth England, Wales and Northern Ireland, London, April 1997, p. 7.

40 Ibid., p. 6.

41 Ibid.

42 *Mining Journal*, London, 23 June 2000.

43 Quoted in *Mining Environmental Management*, London, November 2000.

44 G. McMahon and F. Remy, *Large Mines and the Community*, IDRC, 2001, p. 20.

45 Ibid., p. 24.

46 *World Bank Increasing Social and Environmental Problems*, Press release by CEE Bankwatch Network, 13 December 2005.

47 *IFC's Policy and Performance Standards on Social and Environmental Sustainability and IFC's Disclosure Policy*, IFC/R2006-0010, Washington, DC, 30 January 2006.

48 This summary is based on *A Commentary on World Bank/IFC Proposed Policy and Performance Standards*, published by the Forest Peoples Forum, Moreton-in-Marsh, UK, 3 May 2006.

49 See UN/MONUC, *Report on the conclusions of the Special Investigation into allegations of summary executions and other violations of human rights committed by the FARDC in Kilwa (Province of Katanga) on 15 October 2004.*

50 *Internal Review Slams World Bank over Lapses at Guatemala Mine*, Background paper published by MiningWatch Canada, Friends of the Earth (Canada), the Halifax Initiative (Canada), Bank Information Center (US), 22 August 2005.

51 C. W. Dugger, 'IFC loan for foreign mining in Ghana approved', *New York Times*, 1 February 2006.

52 *Ntostroso Community Attacked*, Press statement, Third World Network Africa, 4 July 2006.

3 | Cursed by resources

'We are in part to blame, but this is the curse of being born with a copper spoon in our mouths.'[1]

It's a startling phenomenon, around which debate has swirled for years: 'lesser-developed' (especially heavily indebted) countries, with a high degree of dependence on mining, display slower rates of economic growth than their peers; some have actually been pushed downwards. Bolivia is the poorest country in Latin America, hosting more big, medium and small-scale mines, proportionate to population, than any other on the subcontinent. Its Potosi region 'has been mined for five centuries, producing a phenomenal amount of silver but at a great human, cultural and environmental cost ... the region around Potosi is one of the poorest in the nation'.[2] Orissa, Bihar and Jharkhand provide the bulk of India's minerals. Yet, for many years, Bihar has been India's 'least developed' state and, in 2005, Orissa was identified by India's National Human Development Report as the poorest in the country. Even in advanced and middle-income countries, it is customarily the most-mined locales that have been the last to share in aggregated wealth. At the onset of the first 'industrial revolution', the English county of Cornwall was the most munificent store of non-ferrous metals anywhere in the world, with 2,000 tin and copper mines operating in 1870. Yet, by the time the last pit closed in 1998, Cornwall had the highest proportion of low-paid workers in the country.[3] Ironically, some of these workers now sell their services to 'nostalgia tourism' – an industry woven around thousands of unreclaimed shafts and abandoned wheelhouses.

It seems to have been Richard Auty who coined the term 'resource curse' in 1993.[4] As early as 1981, however, the United Nations Development Programme (UNDP) had already sounded an alarm on the disproportionate number of mineral-dependent economies (principally in Africa) which were experiencing zero, or even negative, growth. The so-called 'Dutch disease' is also often associated with the 'curse'. In rough outline, this is the economic malaise engendered when a resources boom attracts large amounts of foreign exchange, forcing a drop in the currency exchange rate, followed by resource price volatility and excessive government borrowing. Labour and capital move to the extractive sector away from more sustainable ones, and domestic products no longer prove competitive on international markets.[5]

The curse thesis entered a broader public arena with publication of the World Bank's Extractive Industries Review (EIR) in 2003.[6] The bank acknowledged that, while per capita GDP had been growing by an average of 1.7 per cent in all developing and transitional economies, it was contracting by 2.3 per cent a year in those where minerals accounted for more than 50 per cent of exports.[7] The business of either confirming or rebutting the existence of the phenomenon per se still provides, however, a knotty challenge. On what type of data should we depend? To measure gross domestic product (GDP) just in terms of income from exported extractive resources is deeply suspect. It fails to account for the ways in which that income is domestically distributed, the corrupt internal appropriation of revenues, and parasitic (though legal) state expenditures: building palaces instead of sinking tube wells; fuelling limousines instead of buses and trains. Nor does it define the worth of those resources to future generations, were they left in the ground or upgraded ('value-added') at home rather than offshore. Such wholesale theft of value has, says Professor Patrick Bond, resulted in not only a historical but a 'worsening trap of "primary product" dependence'.[8] Equally important, GDP

44

figures do not, and cannot, evaluate what is lost through the destruction or depreciation of other natural resources within a mining zone: soil fertility, purity of air, quality and quantity of water, fauna and flora.

According to Professor Paul Stevens, 'the key variable to consider is the non-oil, gas or mineral traded GDP, since it is this that must eventually sustain the economy'.[9] But, on its own, that analysis will still fail to account for marked differences in livelihood standards prevailing within a country's borders. Men and women employed directly in mines supported by adequate infrastructure, supplied with reliable power and backed by good health and education facilities, might reasonably manage to put away sufficient savings to fare adequately when the pits close down. But that is a rare prospect for those subsisting at mines elsewhere in the country as casual or migrant labourers. And how do we calculate the loss in development potential for villagers forced to surrender their agricultural land or whose fishing grounds have been blighted with mine wastes?

A more useful tool in determining whether quality of life is improving or declining is the Human Development Index (HDI). Oxfam America finds 'a strong negative correlation between a country's level of mineral dependence and its HDI ranking: the more a state depends on exporting minerals, the *worse* its standard of living is likely to be'.[10] During the 1990s, 'the mineral-dependent states lost ground: the greater a country's level of mineral dependence, the larger the amount it tended to fall in the HDI rankings between 1990 and 1998. The greater the level of dependence, the greater the level of poverty; not only that, but the more difficult it becomes to diversify the economy into more sustainable modes of sustenance and general prosperity.'[11] A 2005 World Bank study tried to ascertain both the replacement costs of water, soil, trees and minerals, and the social consequences of a failure to prevent their depletion. *Where*

45

is the Wealth of Nations? confirms much of what earlier critics have been saying: it's not simply down to good governance to transform mineral wealth into higher standards of living for all citizens. Abatement of poverty is intimately linked to the nature of what is produced, the point in time at which resources are extracted and the methods used. Unfortunately the report has received little attention at large, including from the bank itself (see Chapter 2).[12]

Challenged to provide examples of states that have unequivocally prospered from mineral extraction, industry lobbyists usually cite Australia, Canada and the USA. The contention is dubious on historical grounds alone; when a comparison is made with lesser-developing countries in the present day, it becomes untenable. Australia, the USA and Canada were all endowed (and still are) with massive deposits of ferrous and non-ferrous metals, as well as plentiful coal resources. These served to underpin the early phases of industrialization. Accessing that wealth critically depended on what's often euphemistically dubbed 'internal colonization' – in reality merciless, sometimes ethnocidal, wars to dislodge indigenous communities sitting atop lodes of high-grade minerals.[13] By that time huge quantities of hard coal were being converted into coking coal, iron into steel and copper into electrical wire. Railways, steamships (and, indispensably, armies equipped with bolt-action rifles and machine guns) prefigured extractive projects in South Asia and Latin America which subverted sustainable agriculture for millions of people and cut vast swaths through forests, across plains and over mountains. We are still learning the true costs to the many, exacted by such ventures for the 'betterment' of a comparative few.

Owing partly to this resource theft, there is now no lesser-developing, mineral-rich, state possessing a sufficient and diverse enough storehouse of minerals to pull itself up by its own bootstraps and industrialize to the degree needed to become a competitive global minerals-trading nation. Determined to break free of Western dependency, China, India and Russia did indeed establish their own brands of post-war industrialization; they also enjoyed large and diverse mineral reserves in their own territories (which were traded between each other). But these successes have been bought at an unacceptable socio-ecological price. All three have heavily depended on rampant internal colonization to acquire their mineral wealth: China in Tibet from the 1950s to the present;[14] India, through consistent denial of the constitutional prohibition on transferring Adivasi ('tribal') land to non-tribal persons or private companies;[15] and Russia, with its ruthless appropriation of territory of the officially designated 'small numbered Indigenous Peoples of the Far North'.

Today, these three nations collectively suffer the most insidious ambient air, water and soil pollution on the planet, a major part of which can be directly attributed to mining and minerals processing. Now their own mining companies are sallying forth into Africa, the Asia-Pacific and, to a lesser extent, Latin America, determined to capture new deposits of both metals and fuels. Their mission may not be strictly comparable to those nineteenth- and twentieth-century 'great games' played by Western freebooters. Many of the mines and plants into which they are buying are joint ventures rather than takeovers, while deals are being sealed with Northern companies too. Nevertheless, we might ask whether these forays are morally justifiable when so many of their fellow citizens remain so desperately scarred and blighted by current, and abandoned, mining sites (see Chapter 6).

Are there, then, no erstwhile poverty-stricken states to have achieved a consistent and overall improvement in income and distribution primarily from extracting and marketing their minerals? Two examples are often cited to counter the resource curse trope. The economies of Botswana and Chile are highly dependent on mineral sales and both evince higher standards in health, education and social services than most of their regional neighbours.

Botswana: are diamonds the best of friends?

At first sight, the statistics are impressive. With an exceptional standard rate of growth for a sub-Saharan state,[16] Botswana hosts a small population and boasts an educated elite and a low level of corruption; add to this what Joseph Stiglitz calls the country's 'democratic, consensual and transparent processes'.[17] Until it began major commercial exploitation of its kimberlite (diamondiferous) 'pipes' in the eighties, its GDP was estimated at US$1.1 billion. That had risen nearly tenfold (to US$10.1 billion) by 2005.[18] Nevertheless, despite appearing 'to do all the right things in terms of macro-economic policy to avoid economic overheating and exchange rate appreciation ... mineral rents levelled off in the 1990s and the government's attempts to increase public sector jobs began to look unsustainable as urban unemployment ... began to rise'.[19] It should surely be of some concern that Botswana, to date, has been virtually a 'one-mineral' state. (It does mine some copper and nickel and has potentially economic reserves of uranium.) It possesses, carat for carat, the world's most valuable diamonds, and the government has so far been able to call the shots in negotiations with De Beers, the world's leading diamond marketer. But this will not protect its citizens from a future slump in global diamond demand, and the quality of the gems extracted may soon start to decline.[20] Lately the government has been accused of jeopardizing the sustainable livelihoods of its poorest peoples, the Gana and Gwi ('Bushmen'), by forcibly removing them from their diamond-rich territory. Until now Botswana has actively implemented all the provisions of the Kimberley Process Certification Scheme (KPCS) and is not a source, or transit point, for 'blood' or 'conflict' diamonds. Both the tribal peoples' support group, Survival International, and

Global Witness (the UK organization that effectively launched the Kimberley Process), have, however, urged restrictions on trade in the country's gems should the government continue denying land and other rights to its aboriginal communities.[21] If the KPCS were broadened to include violations of (for example) ILO Convention 169 on Indigenous and Tribal Peoples in Independent Countries, Botswana would be in a double bind: forgo access to the diamonds on Gana and Gwi territory so as to warrant the legitimacy of its output? Or bring those gems to market, and face an international boycott?

Chile: relying on a copper-bottomed future

'Copper flying in the sky, education lying in the soil!'[22]

Chile also enjoys an exceptional status. It has the only world-class mining company to remain in state hands; and possesses the largest single resource of copper. With sales accounting for roughly half the country's exports, few analysts dispute that exploitation of the 'red metal' has been a critical factor in making Chile the fourth-largest economy in Latin America. Marxist president Salvador Allende nationalized all privately owned copper mines, a year after being elected in 1970. Although this was not the only socialist measure to bring him into savage disfavour with the right-wing Chilean opposition, the appropriation rankled most deeply with the United States administration and the huge US copper companies then profiting from exploitations in Chile: Kennecott (now part of Rio Tinto) and Anaconda (bought by Arco in 1977). It is now widely acknowledged that both these companies conspired with the CIA and the communications company ITT, not only in physically disrupting state copper supplies, but backing the bloody coup that toppled Allende in 1973. Perhaps less well known is that dictator Augusto Pinochet did not dismantle the publicly owned copper company Codelco, which had been set up in 1966, partly because the military had its own fingers in that particular pie. The junta also continued to operate an income stabilization fund, under agreement with the World Bank, aimed at offsetting account deficits and paying off national debt.[23] In a recent examination of Chile's rise to relative prosperity, Javier Santino challenges a persistent myth that the critical moment for the country's economic takeoff was the murderous demarche of 1973 and a consequent return to rampant neoliberalization. On the contrary, says Santino, these over-the-top free-market 'principles' propounded by the 'Chicago Boys' (Chileans trained at the Chicago School of Economics to dismantle their state to the limit possible) contributed directly to the catastrophic banking meltdown of 1982. The blunders were confirmed after democracy returned in 1990.[24]

It would still be premature to conclude that Chile has shaken off the spectre of another savage swing from boom to bust, and that Codelco will continue playing the most vital role in ensuring long-term fiscal stability. Professors Richard Auty and Alyson Warhurst reasonably argued in 1993 that 'the sustainable development of a mineral economy ... requires that the mineral sector should be seen not as the backbone of the economy but as a bonus with which to accelerate *competitive* diversification' – in particular 'smoothing sectoral adjustment to shifts in foreign exchange and taxation' through a mineral stabilization fund.[25] If this is the case, then Chileans cannot be sanguine about escaping the pitfalls of the not-too-distant past. Copper remains the main backbone of the Chilean economy and, while the government continues to maintain its mineral stabilization fund, by law 10 per cent of Codelco's earnings are siphoned directly to the military.

Between them, Codelco's Chuquicamata complex and the Escondida mine (owned largely by BHPBilliton, Rio Tinto and Mitsubishi) currently deliver around 16 per cent of copper concentrates to the global market. This makes for a pre-eminent, but far from unassailable, position. (Just as this book was being written, the US giants Freeport and Phelps Dodge announced a friendly merger which would put their copper reserves above those of Codelco.) In mid-2006, Chile began exhibiting signs that the hoary old 'Dutch disease' was creeping into the country's branches, if not yet snatching at its roots. As one financial journalist commented:

> High prices and soaring export revenues from metals have led to a strong appreciation of the peso, undermining the competitiveness of a range of other export products, ranging from wine and grapes to salmon and wood. Exchange rate appreciation ... has aggravated fears that Chile's successful economic model, built on market-friendly reforms, strong public and a broad political consensus, could be running out of steam.[26]

When copper prices reached an unprecedented level in 2005/06 workers inevitably began agitating for a higher percentage of the gains. As BHPBilliton alone chalked up a billion dollars profit that year, its workforce went on strike to demand a greater share of the windfall. The effect was felt within Codelco and both companies eventually made concessions. Meanwhile, students and teachers were vociferously demonstrating on the streets,[27] agitating for a major increase in funding for state schools. Chile's own defence ministry also questioned the armed forces' requisition of such a large chunk of Codelco's bounty, arguing it should go instead towards public health and education. It is a sobering thought that, while Chile is rated seventh best in the world by the World Economic Forum for its 'macro-economy', it lags behind at seventy-sixth for the quality of its overall education, ranking only 100th for its maths and sciences.[28]

Theoretically Chile should have the economic potential to meet the rising social expectations of its citizens. In practice, the government is channelling much of the surplus into two new funds 'designed to take the dollar earnings overseas', rather than exchange them for pesos in the present.[29] It's a World Bank-prescribed 'counter-cyclical' formula that does not augur well for villagers, the poorest citizens in the shanty towns, and the indigenous Mapuche, who continue struggling to gain fundamental rights to their own territory. The tactic may prove somewhat better than the 2006 policy decision, taken by neoliberal Peruvian president Alan Garcia, to allow corporate mining companies to escape higher royalties in exchange for voluntary 'social contributions'. But it stands in marked contrast with recent declarations by presidents Chávez of Venezuela and Morales in Bolivia that they will seize their country's privately owned mines, rather than simply capture a greater share of profits through higher taxes.

The nationalization option

In 2006 there was a ripple of declarations by various governments that they would nationalize, or part-nationalize, private mining enterprises under their jurisdictions. These governments included those of Zimbabwe (although Mugabe was also busy brokering lucrative chrome deals with Chinese companies) and democratic Mongolia. To date, however, the only administration actually to have seized a foreign miner's holdings – lock, stock and barrel – is determinedly anti-democratic Uzbekistan. The regime sequestered Newmont's gold assets in 2006, claiming the US company owed it millions of dollars in back taxes. Much wider attention has been paid to promises made to their electorates by the presidents of Venezuela and Bolivia that they would reverse many years of ruthless foreign exploitation. As yet, neither Hugo Chávez nor Evo Morales has implemented his agenda, and arguably neither ever will. Venezuela's draft mining bill of mid-2006 undertook to 'rescue our sovereignty and nationalise, effectively, mineral resources', by transferring regulation and control to the state and 'promot[ing] the active participation of thousands of small-scale miners, who, for decades, have remained hostage to national and transnational private interests'.[30] In fact, the latter provision was already on Venezuela's statute book, while Chávez's promise to 'rescue sovereignty' seems so far confined to taking back unused mineral leases and forming active joint ventures, rather than compelling companies to surrender their assets altogether. Bolivia's updated Minerals Act, passed in October 2006, also failed to promulgate the return of mine ownership to the public sector. Indeed, Bolivia's vice-president went out of his way to assure companies of 'no need to worry ... private investment, foreign and local ... that generates jobs, won't be touched'.[31] Little wonder, then, that the miners operating in both these countries have breathed deep sighs of relief.

When South-based governments try to substantially alter pre-established investment ground rules, they face considerable odds. Virtually all these states have inherited deals signed on highly favourable terms for foreign companies. For example, under Chile's Statute of Foreign Investment, which 'practically frees [these companies] from any taxes', between 1991 and 2002 the firms paid out around US$160 million; over the same period, Codelco returned ten times as much (US$10.6 billion) to the exchequer.[32] Mining outfits have, on numerous occasions, threatened to sue for compensation for putative 'breaches of contract'. In 2003, several of them told the Indonesian government they would go to international arbitration, were they not granted exemptions to the 1999 Forestry Act, which banned access to their contracts of work in 11 million hectares of protected forest.[33] Despite an outcry from inside parliament and outside, thirteen mining companies got their way. When Mongolia declared in 2005 that it would reassert partial ownership of the country's minerals, more than fifty gold outfits banded together, declaring they would pick up stakes and quit. Shortly afterwards, a newly installed cabinet considerably modified the plan. In 2006,

Canada's Glamis Gold told the Honduran government and residents around its concession in the Siria Valley that 'if it does not get all the concessions it wants to expand its Entre Mares mine, it will shut down early'. As Jamie Kneen of Miningwatch Canada pointed out: 'This would punish the local people who depend on the mine to feed their families, and pit them against the farmers who are trying to get Glamis Gold to take some responsibility for contamination and water scarcity.'[34]

A taxing question

As we saw in the previous chapter, for two decades World Bank/IMF structural adjustment programmes successfully tore apart a wide range of post-colonial taxation systems that were conceived in order to retain mineral-related wealth within poorer countries. The impacts of this attrition are still being felt. Take Tanzania as a recent example. Following passage of its neoliberal Minerals Act in 1997, the East African state swiftly became Africa's third-largest gold producer, after South Africa and Ghana. The World Gold Council and the World Bank both claimed Tanzania's fiscal accounting to be 'a success story'; the bank proudly pointing out that mineral revenues now make up at least half the country's foreign exchange earnings every year. While big miners in Tanzania do pay royalties, they are none the less exempted from the state's 20 per cent value-added tax (VAT) on goods and products used exclusively for mining, and can offset all equipment and machinery costs against their earnings. They are also relieved of corporate taxes until recouping their initial outlays. It's hardly surprising, then, that mining contributes but 3.2 per cent of Tanzania's gross domestic product (GDP). Wages are low (a tenth of the average in South Africa) and foreign companies have been allowed to usurp land previously worked by thousands of small-scale miners, thereby jeopardizing their locally based economies.[35]

This does not mean that mineral-dependent states must knuckle under indefinitely to derisory taxation rules, thus robbing themselves of vital income. In theory a wide variety of measures could be adopted to leverage better returns (rents), while still falling short of a potentially self-destructive act of outright nationalization. These include raising withholding taxes and putting a tax on dividends and upon the mines themselves. Governments might also increase export and import duties, abolish capital allowances, prohibit the offshore retention of earnings and impose 'windfall' taxes during times of larger corporate profit-taking. Perhaps most important, they could abolish tax holidays altogether. But any radical shift towards more equitable income distribution has to be contingent on states collaborating to 'raise the bar' together. Only then may they defeat the industry's determination to 'divide and rule' by playing one government's 'hard' policies off against another's 'softer' ones. Not so far back in time, a few states did own sufficiently large and uniquely high-grade metallic deposits that – at least in theory – they could set their own high prices. Broadly speaking this is no longer the case. South Africa remains the pre-eminent source of platinum, but Russia has sufficient stocks (exactly how much the government refuses to divulge) to give the sub-Saharan state a run for its money in the near future. For many years the Democratic Republic of Congo (former Zaire) dominated world supplies of cobalt. Disruption of mining and supply chains, however, caused by recent murderous conflicts within the country, followed by foreign asset-stripping of the state miner, Gecamines, has seen increasing competitiveness from neighbouring Zambia. With technology available to process this strategic mineral from nickel ores, putative mines like CVRD/Inco's Goro enterprise in New Caledonia, and Chinese-financed Ramu in Papua New Guinea, might soon leave competition from the Democratic Republic of Congo well behind.[36]

Entertaining royalties

In these neoliberalized times, negotiations between miners and states (the predators and their prey) largely focus on fixing royalties. This doesn't mean the industry won't protest if an attempt is made to introduce them for the first time. The Peruvian government tried this in mid-2004 and, not surprisingly, was attacked by Newmont, whose chief gripe was that, since most foreign-owned firms already had signed 'stabilization' agreements, they should be absolved from coughing up new taxes.[37] Soon afterwards, and with a fresh government in place, the proposal was withdrawn.

If a royalty regime is already in place, however, miners and mine ministries usually recognize that they do have to hammer out some kind of compromise. Contemporary rates range, on average, from less than 1 per cent to 3 per cent. They may be applied to profits, gross sales (revenues) or on a deposit's *in situ* value. Companies customarily go for the first option since it is lower than the second. But only the third offers citizens a realistic means to recapture anything approaching the worth of an irreplaceable deposit, once it has been dug up and dispersed. Even so, this does not address the problem of costing that lost resource. Nor does it determine how the proceeds will be distributed among the polity. Few countries where mining plays a significant role have been able to escape conflicting claims between local communities, regional authorities and the central administration over their respective shares of the royalties cake. Last year in India, for instance, the Delhi government proposed a partial *ad valorem* (market price) royalty for its coal-rich states. The states were not impressed and demanded receipt of the total royalty, to be fixed at 20 per cent.[38]

Empowering South Africans?

In 1994, South Africans finally put behind them the insidious legacy of apartheid in all its aspects. Or so most of them believed. The most convincing proof of transformation would lie in transfer of economic power over the country's mineral wealth from white to black hands. For hundreds of thousands of poorer citizens, even more vital would be to reclaim stolen lands, get paid compensation for historical thefts, and finally obtain irreversible legal rights over their subsoil resources. Initially some radicals within the African National Congress (ANC) pushed for blanket public control over all land and what lay beneath it, but it was the 'realists' who came to hold sway over policy implementation. A three-pronged strategy was announced 'to ensure that the state becomes the custodian of the country's mineral wealth and that previously disadvantaged sectors of the population have greater access to that mineral wealth'. But when it finally emerged in late 2002, after seven years of voluble public debate and numerous revisions, the legislation clearly reflected obeisance to the big mining houses, especially Anglo American. The government went out of its way to concede how 'vital' it was 'that, in introducing these sweeping changes, investor confidence does not become a casualty'.[39] The Mineral and Petroleum Resources and Development Act eventually passed into law in October 2002.

Until this stage, private miners had held all mineral rights. Now these rights were to be transferred to the state in a process intended to be completed within five years. During that time companies would continue receiving mining licences, but only on condition that they complied with a new Socio-economic Empowerment Charter, generally known as 'Black Economic Empowerment (BEE)'. Under this innovative legislation, all miners had to ensure that non-white commercial enterprises held at least 15 per cent equity in their companies (again within five years), rising to 26 per cent within a decade. The second policy plank, announced a year later in 2003, was an imposition of royalties varying from 1 to 8 per cent; the highest to be levied on diamonds, while gold and platinum would be assessed at 3 and 4 per cent respectively.[40] The third, potentially most important but divisive, piece of legislation was the granting of land title to tribal communities.

Reactions from the industry were mixed. Some spokespeople approved BEE for its opening up of idle lands to new exploitation and boosting the injection of black capital. Predictably the Chamber of Mines, representing 90 per cent of South Africa's mine owners, argued that introducing royalties would 'quell investment'.[41] After a further three years' delay, and with industry pressure unabating, the final rates were announced towards the end of 2006. Finally, the South African cabinet settled for an average 3 per cent on revenues while the proposed royalties on gold and silver were slashed by half.

Meanwhile 'black empowerment', though potentially a model for both Africa and decolonizing states elsewhere, had failed to fulfil its early promise. The Namibian government, which followed in South Africa's footsteps by introducing 'black empowerment' and a royalties regime similar to its neighbour's, cut the royalty rates by half in November 2006, setting the highest at 3 per cent but with most at only 2 per cent.[42] In 2004 the United Nations Development Programme (UNDP) delivered a scathing report on the early stages of South Africa's Black Economic Empowerment scheme: 'Only a tiny minority of blacks have benefited ... the beneficiaries of these deals belonged largely to the politically well-connected elite ... Overall BEE seems to have entrenched inequality in South Africa. While the incomes of the top 10 per cent of black earners have increased by 30 percent since 1995, the incomes of the bottom 40 percent have decreased in real terms.' Shortly afterwards, Moeletsi Mbeki, brother of the South African president, dubbed BEE a device for 'white-dominated corporations to build bridges with the ANC elite. It doesn't create wealth or add value to the economy.'[43]

The National Union of Mineworkers went a step farther, accusing UK-based Lonmin (formerly Lonhro) of setting up a BEE partner, Incawala Resources, primarily to recycle its own debt. Appointed as chair of Incawala was Brian Gilbertson, a consultant to Lonmin, recently the chairman of Vedanta Resources plc, and former head of Gencor, one of South Africa's most intransigent companies during the apartheid era. At least two men have become 'rand billionaires' as a result of BEE. One of these, Patrice Motsepe, heads African Rainbow Minerals (ARM), Anglo American's close partner in the Modikwa joint venture at Maandagshoek, where the farming community last year suffered an attack disturbingly reminiscent of the former days of sufferance under white rule.

Box 3.1 Black Friday at Monday's Corner

On Friday 9 June 2006 – exactly forty years after the Soweto students' uprising – another crowd of black South African protesters were fired upon by police. They too were unarmed and shot in the back. Twenty-six people were taken to local hospitals, eight with rubber-bullet wounds. Another patient was struck in the arm by live ammunition, requiring removal of the bullet. The victims were poor black farmers from a small community in the north-eastern province of Mpumalanga, called Maandagshoek (literally 'Monday's Corner'). They were trying to stop encroachment on their land by Anglo American, whose Anglo Platinum (Amplats) subsidiary had ordered police to break up the protest.

Anglo American leads the world in delivering platinum and much of it is under the farms around Maandagshoek. The amount of platinum contained in a tonne of ore averages 4–7 grams, so between 7 and 12 tonnes of rock must be dug up and dumped for every ounce of final product. Around Anglo's mines, waste rock and tailings piles rise five storeys high. Uncovered, unvegetated and uncontoured, their potentially damaging content is continually blowing in the wind.

The inhabitants of Maandagshoek live on the edge of a vast, saucer-shaped metal-rich plateau called the Bushveldt. Their ploughing and grazing fields are directly in the path of expansion by the Modikwa mine, owned by Anglo Platinum and its BEE partner, African Rainbow Minerals, along with two 'community companies'. For some years they had been in dispute with Anglo Platinum over what they claimed to be their constitutional right to exclusive use and enjoyment of portions of the land. In its encroachment, the company has caused significant damage to property and harm to the environment, allegedly damaging crops and community groundwater resources, releasing contaminated mine water, polluting surface water and dumping large quantities of waste rock on to the land. Anglo Platinum also forced a number of farmers off their lands when it established its mine infrastructure.

The company was asked by the community to respect its rights: if it required access, it should obtain a court order. According to the community's lawyer, Richard Spoor: 'Anglo declined to approach the court out of concern that it might uphold the community's property rights. Such a decision would have enormous consequences for Anglo Platinum and other mining companies operating on tribal land.' It was, says Mr Spoor, only when Anglo refused to respect their property rights that the community resolved on a more direct approach.

On 9 June, officers from a nearby police station arrived at

the drill site to arrest three community leaders, but without authorization to detain anyone else. A crowd of local people had already gathered at the site and was ordered to disperse. When they refused, they were fired upon with rubber bullets and a pistol.

Maandagshoek community members have enjoyed beneficial occupation of those farms for generations – certainly since well before Anglo Platinum bought them, according to Richard Spoor. 'Their rights are protected by the law and by the constitution. Anglo Platinum may insist that the black empowerment companies have consented to its mining activities on tribal land. It does so despite the fact that the directors of these companies are overwhelmingly supportive of the Maandagshoek community's struggle to have its indigenous land rights respected and that they expressly disavow the company's authority to represent, much less to bind, indigenous communities in respect of those rights. The central demand of the Maandagshoek community is that the mine agree to negotiate terms of access to tribal land which regulate compensation for the loss and harm the community will suffer as a result of mining activities, and issues relating to the protection of the environment and rehabilitation. Anglo Platinum refuses to negotiate these issues and chooses instead the route of confrontation and repression. The company is waging a war on the community, on their culture, their traditions, their leaders, their environment and their way of life.'

For its part Anglo Platinum claimed that its BEE partners fully supported its position and that the protesters were unrepresentative of the community as a whole. Nine days after the 9 June shootings, however, more than six hundred local women and men, along with a representative of one of the two smaller BEE partners in the Modikwa joint venture, met under a Marula tree. There, they unanimously resolved to step up resistance to the company's encroachment on its fields and roads, organize a protest march and take their grievances directly to the UK conglomerate's 'big boss', Sir Mark Moody-Stuart. As of November 2006, Anglo American had failed to resolve any of the issues raised by the communities of Maandagshoek.[44]

South African tribal peoples' indigenous title is supposedly guaranteed by Section 25 of the Constitution (the 'property clause') and provisions of the Interim Protection of Informal Land Rights Act of 1996. While the legislation doesn't enshrine a community's right to exercise 'fully informed prior consent' to the use of its traditional land, none the less the intent is clear. A major gulf has developed, however, between this legal promise and any meaningful implementation. According to South African human rights lawyer Richard Spoor: 'Mining companies claim they already have permits to drill and mine on tribal land without permission of the immediate community and without paying compensation directly to its members; even without going to court to enforce a supposed possession order.'[45] It is this conflict between two sets of 'rights' (one trampled on; the other arguably spurious) which has so far stymied any realistic prospect of a significant economic revival in several parts of the country. Regrettably there is little indication that the government is willing to take on the big miners rather than take up the peoples' cause. The Nama of Richtersveld went to Johannesburg's constitutional court in 2003 to reclaim land and diamond rights potentially worth billions of dollars. They were robbed of their land back in the nineteenth century and had been forced to subsist under tin roofs, without access to electricity. The court ruled that the Nama had been victimized by 'racist laws' and enjoyed a legitimate claim to ownership.

Despite this, the ANC government strenuously resisted surrendering the concessions, arguing that 'the greater good is served by sharing the diamond wealth with the nation'. Alexkor, which held the lease, added insult to injury by claiming the Nama were 'too uncivilised to own land'. This thoroughly reprehensible allegation is compounded by the fact that Alexkor is a state-owned corporation. Finally, in October 2006, the Nama won an out-of-court settlement. The struggle had lasted more than a century, during which the tribe endured abject poverty.[46]

What is the true wealth of nations?

When we talk of 'mineral wealth' we tend to assume that copper, gold, diamonds and so forth possess (like land) a fixable monetary worth. But minerals can never be returned to their original state and therefore – almost paradoxically – their true value can only be derived from assessing what has been lost, sometimes called the 'cost of replacement'. Jeremy Richards of the University of Alberta Department of Earth and Atmospheric Sciences has proposed that such costs should be set by international agreement, commencing with minimum royalty rates on revenues, not profits, 'and that these should be slowly increased over several years to allow markets time to adjust'. Thus, 'consumers would be made directly aware of the irreplaceable value of minerals and metals, leading to a change in usage patterns, and the benefits of resource extraction would be more equitably distributed to producer nations'.[47] It's a noble proposal, but not particularly new: attempts by mineral-rich states to set up producer–consumer commodity pacts during the 1970s foundered on the withdrawal of backing from developed states.

Assessing this true value does not simply mean gauging future profits that might be had by leaving deposits in the ground until market prices rise. Crucially it requires a system under which the taxes, wages, infrastructure and socio-economic enterprises financed by a mine are set against the costs of polluted rivers, barren soil, dislocated local businesses, occupational diseases and a host of other variables. The calculation must also include hidden subsidies provided by the host state to miners, such as the provision of cheap electrical power, railheads and irreplaceable water bodies.

Debates over the nature and dimensions of the 'resources curse' often stray into hyperbole or generalizations that ignore the critical reality of what mining does to people in 'intentional' or self-chosen communities. Analysts tend to show more concern with what mineral over-dependence may do to government exchequers and their need to balance the books. So long as the states have established some form of stability fund and fixed long-term contracts, it might seem that they can mine as much as they want when both spot and futures prices are high and costs can be underwritten by foreign direct investment. But bitter histories teach more than a few lessons on how better to cope with the 'bulls and bears'. They show that ripping up the earth destroys not only the commons but, if allowed to proceed simply as a strategy to secure a market edge, may strike at the fabric of sustainability. Last July, India's influential *Financial Express* examined the possible economic consequences of the nation's current iron ore 'rush', which has been bearing down most heavily on the predominantly Adivasi (tribal) regions of Orissa, Jharkhand and Chhattisgarh. The newspaper concluded that opening wide the door to mostly foreign enterprises was not principally prompted by India's requirements for its own internal growth. Rather it was due to the interventions of global steel manufacturers, thirsting for cheap raw materials to feed their offshore and onshore plants. Warned the newspaper: '[D]omestic demand will have to rise to over 13% every year from today to 2020', in order to absorb the projected output.' If all the deals now on the table were to materialize, 'the country's iron ore could be exhausted in just fifty years'.[48] While it is highly unlikely that all the mining projects now on the drawing board in India will make it to production, this will not spare hundreds of rural communities from further incursions on to their land. Within two generations, numerous sustainable – and already fragile – livelihoods will have been sacrificed, and India as a whole will have lost too.

Notes

1 Kenneth Kaunda, former president of Zambia, cited in M. Ross, 'The political economy of the resource curse', in *World Politics*, 51, January 1999, p. 297.

2 *Breaking New Ground: Mining, Minerals and Sustainable Development: The Report of the MMSD Project*, Earthscan, London, 2002, p. 232.

3 S. Payne, B. Henson, D. Gordon and R. Forrest, 'Poverty and deprivation in West Cornwall in the 1990s', Statistical Monitoring Unit, School for Policy Studies, 2006, p. 6.

4 R. Auty, *Sustaining Development in Mineral Economies: The Resource Curse Thesis*, Routledge, London, 1993.

5 S. Pegg, 'Poverty reduction or poverty exacerbation? World Bank group support for extractive industries in Africa', Report sponsored by Oxfam America, Friends of the Earth-US, Environmental Defense, Catholic Relief Services and the Bank Information Centre, 2003, p. 15; K. Lahiri-Dutt, '"May God give us chaos, so that we can plunder": a critique of "resource curse" and conflict theories', *Development*, Society for International Development, Rome, September 2006, 49(3): 15.

6 P. Stevens, 'Resource impact: a curse or a blessing?' (in draft), CEPMLP, Dundee, 2003, p. 4.

7 Pegg, 'Poverty reduction', p. 14.

8 P. Bond, 'Multinational capital's responsibility for Africa's resource extraction crisis', Paper for the Open Society Initiative for Southern Africa, 2006, p. 13.

9 Stevens, 'Resource impact', p. 6.

10 M. Ross, 'Extractive sectors and the poor', Oxfam America, 2001, p. 8.

11 Ibid.

12 *Where is the Wealth of Nations? Measuring Capital for the 21st Century*, World Bank, Washington, DC, 2005.

13 For graphic descriptions of this process in Australia, see J. Roberts, *Massacres to Mining: The Colonisation of Aboriginal Australia*, Dove Communications, Blackburn (Australia), 1981; D. W. McLeod, *How the West was Lost* (self-published), Port Hedland, Australia, 1984. A good US backgrounder is A. Gedicks, *New Resource Wars: Native and Environmental Struggles*, South End Press, Boston, MA, 1993.

14 Tibet Information Service, 'Mining Tibet: mineral exploitation in Tibetan areas of the PRC', London, 2002.

15 This fundamental right, established by Schedule V of India's 1947 Constitution, was almost universally ignored until the historic Supreme Court 'Samatha Judgment' of 1997 issued against the state of Andhra Pradesh. The ruling blocked the Aditya Birla mining company from exploiting deposits of calcite and other construction materials on tribal territory. Although the judgment should have been enforced through India as a whole, it has been ignored or rejected by almost every state. One rare exception was the recently promulgated 'tribal' state of Chhattisgarh. In 2001 its government challenged a decision by the central government to permit a takeover by the Sterlite company of state-controlled Bharat Aluminium Company (BALCO), stating that this would violate the Samatha Judgment. The Supreme Court then went back on its previous ruling, permitting the transfer of thousands of hectares of Adivasi land to Sterlite – now Vedanta Resources plc, registered in London. See R. Rebbapragada and K. Bhanumathi, 'The Fifth Schedule of the Indian Constitution and the Samatha Judgment', *Indigenous Law Bulletin*, Sydney, November/December 2001, 5(13): 22–3. For further details on Vedanta in Chhattisgarh, see 'Ravages through India: Vedanta Resources plc counter report', published by Nostromo Research, London and India Resource Center, San Francisco, CA, August 2005, p. 5.

16 World Bank, *Where is the Wealth of Nations?*, p. 66.

17 J. Stiglitz, 'We can now cure Dutch disease', *Guardian*, London, 18 August 2004.

18 World Bank Group, 'Botswana at a glance', Washington, DC, 11 August 2006.

19 Stevens, 'Resource impact', p. 11.

20 'Looking for the via media in Botswana', interview with Dr Robert Hitchcock, Professor of Anthropology at the Department of Anthropology and Geography in the University of Nebraska, *Indian Minerals & Metals Review*, April 2006.

21 See 'We support the Kimberley process', *Mwegi*, Gaberone, 10 October 2006; also Janine Roberts, 'Masters of illusion: special report

on the Bushmen of the Kalahari', *Ecologist*, London, September 2003, pp. 34–43.

22 This was one of the chants of the National Student Strike, held in Chile on 30 May 2006.

23 S. Tali, *Caspian Oil Windfalls: Who will Benefit?*, Open Society Institute, New York, 2003.

24 See J. Santino, *Latin America's Political Economy of the Possible: Beyond Good Revolutionaries and Free Marketeers*, MIT Press, Boston, MA, 2006.

25 R. Auty and A. Warhurst, 'Sustainable development in mineral exporting economies', *Resources Policy*, London, March 1993, 19(1): 29.

26 R. Lapper, 'Copper boom prompts Chile to save now and spend later', *Financial Times*, 18 May 2006.

27 D. Kosich, 'Chilean mining union seeks 5% wage hike, large bonus', *Mineweb*, 13 October 2006.

28 D. Kosich, 'Record copper revenues will go to help Chile's social programs', *Mineweb*, 6 October 2006.

29 Lapper, 'Copper boom'.

30 Quoted by D. Kosich, 'Muy rápido Venezuela mining law reform on agenda', *Mineweb*, 19 June 2006.

31 D. Kosich, 'Bolivia's President cries "nationalisation" again while ministers insist mining has nothing to fear', *Mineweb*, 17 October 2006.

32 'How much do mining companies contribute?', *Noticias Alindos*, 27 January 2005.

33 'Public outcry over mining threat to Indonesian protected forests', Press statement, Mineral Policy Institute, Australia, 23 June 2003.

34 J. Kneen, 'The social licence to mine: passing the test', Presentation to the Round Table on Corporate Social Responsibility, Montreal, Miningwatch Canada, Ottawa, 14 November 2006.

35 Tom Maliti, 'Miners begin to feel the rumblings from tax-starved Tanzania', Associated Press report, 30 October 2006.

36 See *Cobalt News*, published by the Cobalt Development Institute, Guildford (UK), January 2006, p. 8.

37 W. Gluschke, 'Peru sets new royalty rates', *Mineweb*, 7 June 2004.

38 G. Maxumdar, 'States reject coal royalty formula', *Hindustan Times*, Ranchi, 1 March 2006.

39 S. Pratt, 'South Africa's geological gifts', *Geotimes*, December 2003.

40 Minerals and Petroleum Royalties Bill, introduced to parliament by the South African minister of finance on 10 March 2003.

41 Pratt, 'South Africa's geological gifts'.

42 See 'Namibia reduces planned royalties', *Mining Journal*, 17 November 2006. There is one important difference between the royalties

set by South Africa and those set by Namibia. The South African government has kept some rates in the lower percentile in order to encourage companies to beneficiate (in other words process) their output, and keep some of their profits, within South Africa. In contrast, Namibia plans to apply its rates across the board, whether or not minerals are delivered in a raw, semi-processed or processed form. At the time of writing it is not clear whether South Africa's policy will secure more benefit for the country than Namibia's. This largely depends on how the companies react in the medium term.

43 United Nations Development Programme (UNDP), 'Cultural liberty in today's diverse world', 2004.

44 R. Moody, 'Black Friday at Monday's Corner', *Mines and Communities*, 24 June 2006.

45 Cited in ibid.

46 *Guardian*, London, 13 October 2006.

47 J. Richards, '"Precious Metals": the case for treating metals as irreplaceable', Abstract, *Journal of Cleaner Production*, 14, p. 324.

48 *Financial Express*, Mumbai, 15 July 2006.

4 | Blood, toil and tears

Jobs in mining account for between 0.5 and 1 per cent of global employment. In 1990, around 25 million workers were officially registered to the industry (and 10 million in coal alone). According to the International Labour Organization (ILO), however, by 2000 at least 5.5 million previously secure jobs had been lost – no fewer than 3.2 million of them in the five years before the turn of the century.[1] These are certainly underestimates, since some key mineral-dependent states (among them Chile, Russia, Peru and Zambia) had not been included in the survey, nor were workers at processing plants and in many small-scale mines. If we add family members involved in ancillary activities, unregistered or casual labourers in quarries and those transporting or trading mined materials, the number of those dependent on mining would probably top 200 million.

The sobering reality is that, although formal employment in the sector has markedly fallen in many countries over the past decade and a half, the proportion of ill-paid, disempowered, subcontracted mineworkers has significantly increased. Some of them will be hired directly by mine management, but most will be local people or poor migrants, taken on when a project is under construction, and the main aptitudes required are driving a JCB or truck, digging trenches and installing elementary structures. Once the mine is close to coming 'on-stream' the majority of these workers will get sacked; something rarely reflected in those frequent company promises to 'bring much-needed employment' to a depressed area.[2]

Training in durable skills costs time and money and, in recent times, the white- and blue-collar labour pool has begun running dry. All major mine operators will try to cut production expenses and boost output: substituting machines for humans, and switching to open-cast excavation (or 'block caving') from underground tunnelling are typical ways of doing so. When the US coal king Massey Energy adopted 'mountain-top removal' (literally bulldozing hill peaks and dumping wastes directly into valleys and streams) it cost the livelihoods of hundreds of shaft miners in the rest of Appalachia. On average US strip coal mines produce up to a third more coal per worker than their underground counterparts. Between 1979 and 2003 more than half the regional mine workforce was 'wiped out'.[3]

Cost-cutting isn't always the prime motive behind 'retrenchment'. Sensible precautions by Canada's Cameco led to the introduction of electronically guided robots to gouge out potentially deadly grades of uranium from the world's biggest uranium mine, McArthur, in Saskatchewan. Nevertheless, storms flooded one of the pits, releasing water rich in radon gas in 2004. Workers were sent underground without protective respirators in order to 'save the mine and their jobs' (*sic*). Cameco claimed that employees could work more effectively without being hampered by safety gear and that radiation exposures were 'well below the prescribed limit'.[4]

Britain's National Union of Mineworkers saw a 1981 membership of 250,000 razed to just over 5,000 in twenty years.[5] Arguably, the deep mines could have operated profitably for years to come (albeit at reduced strength). But the attrition was politically inspired: a direct consequence of the Thatcher government's determination to privatize the coal industry and break the National Union of Mineworkers' radical backbone. Similar motives have played a major role in deunionization strategies elsewhere. From 1996 onwards, Rio Tinto methodically set out to prune workforces at its coal mines in Australia in order to put a brake on industrial action aimed at better health and safety standards. The powerful

CFMEU (Construction, Forestry, Mining and Engineering Union) became a sworn enemy of the company's ruthless determination to do away with collective bargaining.[6] In the face of the company's intransigence, the union went on to establish a unique global Rio Tinto campaign network, under the auspices of the ICEM (International Federation of Chemical, Energy, Mine and General Workers' Unions). In 1999 the ICEM extended this corporate campaign to target three Canadian companies: Placer Dome, for retrenchment of 40 per cent of its South African workforce; Inco, because of an arbitrary lock-out of a thousand workers; and Goldcorp, for its attempted scrapping of a thirty-five-year-old collective bargaining agreement.[7] Until India announced the privatization of some of its public industries (PSUs) from 1993 onwards, successive governments had largely protected workers from arbitrary dismissal, adhering to policies laid down at the country's independence in 1947. But, as more operations get ceded to the private sector, so more jobs have been lost.

With the exception of Ecuador, Brazil and Papua New Guinea, most key mineral-dependent states reporting to the ILO between 1985 and 2000 revealed a disturbing extent of dismissals. During those fifteen years, roughly half of South African, Bolivian and Australian employees had lost their jobs; in India the official workforce went down by 14 per cent. At the same time, more mines were adopting a twelve-hour shift system, adding to fears of an increase in accidents and exposure to hazardous dust. Contractual employment dropped slightly in Australia and India between 1995 and 2000, but almost doubled in Ukraine.[8]

Since the dawn of the new millennium, a few states have reported a substantial increase in employment, notably Mexico (257,000 workers in 2006) and Peru (70,000). But, in fact, many employees are recruited as 'independent' or temporary labourers. According to a September 2006 report by the Comisión Económica para América Latín y el Caribe (CEPAL/ECLAC), the current trend in most of South and Central America is towards 'an increase in non-unionised workers, because the mining companies use subcontracted workers as part of their cost controls, avoiding the financial burden of providing benefits'.[9] Reliable data are not available from China or India for the much larger legions of unregistered or 'illegal' miners in quarrying and coal. Here, even large, publicly registered companies themselves may under-report their true dependence on underpaid labourers recruited from outside (see Chapter 5).

Challenged to identify the worst impacts of mining, many of us will reach into our own family histories or iconic images drawn from the past: the breadwinner crushed by a rock fall at a local stone quarry; homes swept away under an avalanche of slurry. But empathy alone cannot measure the true scale of mine workplace injuries, nor the scarcely visible consequences for millions of occupational disability brought on by silicosis, pneumoconiosis, asbestosis, hearing loss or being constantly subjected to machine vibration.[10]

If we trust government statistics, the number of accidents at formal mines has steadily diminished over recent years. Progress has varied from country to country, however, depending on technology used, type of mineral extracted, vigilance of employers, and above all the amount of money set aside to improve working conditions. Owing to its deep mining tradition, South Africa has a much higher fatality rate than Australia, the USA and Canada. In 2005, the South African Department of Minerals and Energy recorded the accidental deaths of 202 mineworkers. Although this marked a decrease (from 246 deaths in 2004, and 270 the year before) it was the bigger, ostensibly better-managed mines which were responsible for almost 80 per cent of these fatalities, demonstrating that 'neither large nor small mines can say they have cracked the code for zero fatalities'.[11]

Despite Australia's better safety record, and a cut in fatalities of 50 per cent since 1996, a down-under miner is still twice as likely to die as any other worker (5 deaths per 100,000 workers as against 2.3 per 100,000).[12] Digging in a US underground mine constitutes the deadliest occupation after forestry, farming and commercial fishing. Safety improvements during the 1990s failed to prevent the loss of twelve lives at the privately run Sago coal mine in January 2006 – the worst accident of its kind for four years. Just five years earlier, the Bush administration had scrapped the introduction of seventeen updated safety regulations.[13] In the nine months succeeding this disaster, forty-two miners lost their lives[14] – this was almost double the total fatalities for the previous year.[15]

If you're an Indian mineworker the chance of dying is almost four times greater than if you're employed in any other industry. Officially, the rate has gone down in recent years and now stands at one hundred a year.[16] This is a grotesque underestimate: according to a study by Direct Initiatives for Social Health and Action (DISHA), based in the eastern mining city of Asansol, every year around three hundred large-scale accidents occur at illegal mines along the West Bengal–Jharkhand coal belt, claiming the lives of at least two thousand miners. 'In most cases the deaths go unreported because of a police–mafia nexus.'[17] In 2006, the government claimed that the nation's mine safety record had 'improved over time', while conceding that 'mine disasters ... happen ... with disconcerting regularity, mostly in underground mines' and 'the scourge of inundation has increased alarmingly in the recent past'. Yet, just as this report was off the press, a single explosion, at the state-owned Bhatdih coal mine in Jharkhand, took the lives of fifty-four men.[18]

The toll of coal

Coal mineworkers have forged historical movements for social change all over the globe. It was the National Union of Mineworkers which headed Britain's first (and so far only) General Strike of 1926. Two and a half decades later, in 1953, thousands of prisoners in the Siberian 'gulag' laid down tools in protest at the appalling conditions in and around Vorkuta's coal pits. One historical commentator has called this revolt 'the first effective challenge to Stalinism'. According to Raya Dunayevskaya (the principal theorist of 'state capitalism', who founded Marxist humanism), it destroyed the myth that the Soviet system was invincible and, though met with savage retribution by Stalin's troops, led directly to the eventual emptying of the forced labour camps.[19]

Underground coal shafts harbour more dangers, and claim more 'accident' victims, than all other underground mines put together. Yet this bitter truth rarely gets entered into calculations of the full impacts of our continued global dependence on the 'black stuff'. Risks of explosions from 'firedamp' (methane) and carbon monoxide poisoning have been recorded (if not properly diagnosed) for at least two hundred years. In May 1812, a methane explosion raked the Felling Colliery in the British county of Durham, sending fires along two shafts and causing the deaths of ninety-two workers.[20] Recognized as a major calamity at the time, the disaster has passed into UK labour folklore.[21] Almost two centuries later, in November 2004, nearly twice that number of workers (166) died from a similar gas explosion at the Chenjiashan coal mine in China's Shanxi province. Several hundred angry, distraught and bereaved relatives and friends then stormed the colliery and local government offices, accusing officials of failing to reveal the genuine death toll, and of intimidating journalists against reporting the event. Worse, only a year later, another methane blast at the Dongfeng colliery in the country's north-east killed 171 miners. According to China Watch (a project set up by the World Watch Institute, Washington, DC): '[M]ine managers were not even aware of the central government's emergency regulations. Such ignorance of work safety, pollution, and educational needs – the underlying cause of thousands of tragedies – exists widely in Chinese industries.'[22]

Chinese authorities reported in 2002 that around 60 per cent of all the country's industrial deaths were caused by coal mining, bearing financial losses as high as US$180 million per annum. Three years later, the government itself acknowledged that coal mine accidents in the country account for 80 per cent (*sic*) of the world's total.[23] Back in 1998, when the death rate was officially reported to be an impossibly low 10,000, the regime had already ordered the closure of more than 25,000 small mines.[24] Many of these, however, reopened elsewhere, almost as soon as they were put out of action. Six years later, in 2004, the regime set up a Bureau for Supervising Coal Mine Safety, promising to dispatch supervisory agencies to oversee the country's major mines and close down minor pits not found up to standard. The strategy clearly did not work because, in August the following year, the authorities once more ordered the shutting of 7,000 mines; and yet again a large number were reported to be back in production within a week.[25] Only three months later, a further 12,000 mines were ordered to suspend production.[26] Statistics released in the first week of 2006 did suggest a slight improvement in coal mine safety. But, on deconstructing the aggregate figures, it became apparent that large-scale disasters had actually become more frequent, killing two to three times as many people as in the year before. In response, the Hong Kong-based labour rights group, China Labour Bulletin (CLB), called on the authorities 'to reform the current work safety supervision system and allow miners themselves to organize their own work safety teams and take part directly in safety supervision'.[27] To date, the plea has fallen on deaf ears. On 14 November 2006, CLB announced that yet another 104 coal workers had been killed in a series of disasters across the country over the previous eight days.[28]

Attempts by Chinese employees to gain compensation follow-ing such dire events often become grounded, not only on the reefs of bureaucracy, but also on the sandbanks of administrative paranoia. Human rights lawyer Gao Zhisheng helped relatives of workers killed in the 2004 Chenjiashan coal mine explosion to launch suits, seeking up to 1 million yuan (around US$125,000) in damages for each victim. While embarking on these and similar cases, Zhisheng was officially ordered to stop practising for a year. 'For three days after the accident they did not send anyone down to clear the blocked pits and save the miners,' declared Zhisheng. 'Neither did they provide a living allowance for miners' families.' A manager at the colliery admitted to CLB that the high death toll was a result of officials 'illegally forcing miners down the pits for more than 10 hours a day, 7 days a week, being paid just 700 yuan [less than US$200] a month'.[29]

Finally in 2006 the ILO published a new safety code for the global coal sector, twenty years after the previous one. The code includes a methodology for identifying hazards which covers flammable coal dust and fires,[30] and inrushes of water and gas, among other issues. The new code is voluntary, however, and fails to bind those governments that sign up to it.

Dying for a living
Asbestosis and related diseases Asbestos products wipe out the lives of at least 100,000 people every year, and the rate is rising. Although global production of the deadly material has fallen since the 1970s, increasing numbers of workers in the USA, Canada, the UK, Germany and other industrialized countries are now dying from past exposure to asbestos dust. Equally (if not more) disturbing is that millions of people in the global South, especially in China, India, Thailand and Indonesia, face daily contact with these carcinogenic fibres in their homes, fac-tories, schools and public buildings. Many, so far unrecognized

as sufferers, will fall victim to mesothelioma, asbestosis and asbestos-related pleural disease within the next two decades. Just how many mineworkers (as distinct from members of the general population) are fated to contract these fatal diseases in the near future is almost anyone's guess. While the rate of extracting blue and brown asbestos seems to have dropped to almost nothing, the 'white' (chrysotile) variety continues to be peddled from mines in Russia and Canada. Scandalously, the Canadian government continues to boost chrysotile exports, claiming – against all evidence and an emphatic ILO resolution of 2006 – that it is safe.[31]

Bringing asbestos manufacturing companies to book has been fraught with problems. Some manufacturers have lately settled claims with reasonable expediency, but insurance companies continue squabbling among themselves over who bears the ultimate responsibility for paying compensation.[32] Mining companies have proved even more recalcitrant. In June 2003, Cape plc and Gencor finally settled with 7,300 South African miners and residents – to the tune of £10.67 million – for asbestosis and related injuries caused by the companies' operations up until nine years earlier (although Cape had started mining the deadly material as far back as 1893).[33] US-based WR Grace managed to escape indictment for many years until, late last year, it was ordered by the Supreme Court to pay US$14 million to clean asbestos from its vermiculite mine at Libby in Montana. Although the court warned that criminal charges were likely to be filed against seven of Grace's present and former chief executives,[34] claims for compensation by 200 mineworkers and their dependants remain pending.[35]

Silicosis, pneumoconiosis, emphysema Asbestos is often described as the world's leading 'industrial killer'. This is probably true for North America and western Europe. Silicosis runs it a close second in many other countries, however, and may soon be confirmed as the world's worst industrial hazard. The ILO says that silicosis 'still affects tens of millions of workers around the world. In Latin America, 37% of miners have some degree of the disease, rising to 50% among miners aged over 50. In India, over 50% of slate pencil workers and 36% of stonecutters have silicosis.'[36] But companies continue to grossly minimize its significance.[37] One hindrance to scaling the problem is that silicosis is widely misdiagnosed as tuberculosis: the latter is usually curable, the former almost invariably ends in death. Some estimates put the number of victims at half a million in South Africa alone.[38] It was not until 2004 that serious efforts were made to bring offending companies to court for failure to prevent silicosis in their gold mines, when ten former employees filed a test case against Anglo American plc. Two years later, the miners were still waiting for their days in court. An industry spokesperson acknowledged that even the minimum goal of establishing limits to occupational silicosis – which affect diamond as well as gold workers – was not likely to be met by the target date of 2008.[39] The Chinese authorities have likewise declared that pneumoconiosis (of which silicosis and coal workers' 'black-lung disease' are the most prevalent forms) is the single worst occupational illness in the country today, accounting for as much as 80 per cent of all industrial incapacitation. There have been more than 580,000 cases of pneumoconiosis registered since the 1950s, with some 140,000 people officially recognized to have succumbed. Owing to widespread lack of health check-ups, '[e]xperts estimate that the actual number of cases is around ten times higher'. In addition, '[a] further 10,000 or so new [silicosis cases] are currently emerging each year ... All the signs indicate that, as a side effect of the country's rapid economic development, the scale of the occupational silicosis epidemic in China is getting worse each year.'[40] A December 2005 study of the epidemic among a group

Box 4.1 A collapse of credibility

Two Papua New Guinean workers lost their lives during a landslide at the Lihir gold mine in October 2005. In the constellation of such occurrences it seemed a minor event (except, of course, to the victims' families and relatives). What sets it apart is that, although the company called the collapse 'a natural disaster', it had been eminently predictable. Lihir Gold's prospectus, published thirteen years before, conceded Lihir island to be seismically unstable, having registered several earthquakes up to 7.5 on the Richter scale since the early 1900s. For this reason, and owing to the paucity of land for waste storage, a system of piping wastes into the ocean (submarine tailings disposal) was selected. Rio Tinto operated the mine until a month before the disaster. It knew full well that one of the project investors, Credit Suisse First Boston, had warned a full year before that: 'One must question the safety of other areas until now assessed as geo-technically stable.'[41] Even more disturbing, Rio Tinto was also jointly responsible, as junior partner to Freeport McMoran, when a similar, but far bigger, landslide took the lives of eight Papuan workers at their Grasberg mine in West Papua, only two years before.

of jewellery workers in Guangdong suggested that 'the denial of compensatory justice to workers who contract silicosis and related occupational illnesses is often a result of collusion between business interests, local government, hospitals and the courts, which have a shared interest in downplaying the seriousness'.[42]

Displaying many of the symptoms of pneumoconiosis, but requiring a distinct diagnosis and pattern of treatment, is emphysema, which strikes at the upper respiratory tract. In 1997, Britain's High Court ordered the former state mining company British Coal to pay compensation to 100,000 ex-miners with emphysema, chronic obstructive airway disease, chronic pulmonary disease and chronic bronchitis. The company woefully ignored the order and, in 2000, the UK government very belatedly stepped in to provide extra cash. Since the original court ruling, some six thousand miners had died without receiving any compensation whatsoever;[43] hundreds of mineworkers, suffering from the effects of 'vibration white finger', were already excluded from the original judgment.[44]

Working women

'Mining is seen as so "naturally" masculine that few people consider its effects on women. What they don't realise is that the low-cost labour of Third World men as miners is sustained and subsidised by unpaid female labour; in the household, on farms and at markets.'[45]

An ILO report on employment in the organized mining sector, published in 2002, remarked that 'Mining remains a male-dominated industry, perhaps for good reason [*sic*]. The proportion of women in the workforce in a sample of 15 countries varies from about 1 per cent to 25 per cent. Female employment is typically below 10 per cent and has changed little in the 15 years between 1985 and 2000.'[46] Some administrations, including those in Indonesia and China, ban female mine labour altogether; others (including India's) allow women to work above, but not beneath, the ground. In South Africa and the USA, a woman's right to stand shoulder to shoulder with males has been achieved only after long and hard battles with both governing authorities and their own menfolk. 'Despite all the risks, the women are determined. Mining gives them opportunities they have never had before and they're desperate to keep their jobs. [The] companies want to attract women because they make good, reliable workers.[47] (This sentiment may well be echoed by South Africa's Anglo American Corporation, which, in October 2006, appointed the first female chief executive officer ever to head a major mining company.)

According to the ILO: 'In most countries and companies the average remuneration of women in mining is below that of men; the representation of women in senior management positions is less than that of men; and the average turnover of female employees in mining is higher than that of males.' The UN body goes on to claim that 'this situation is no different from that in many other economic sectors, public and private, in many countries. But increasing numbers of mining companies are taking measures, either voluntarily or as a result of legislation to counter these imbalances. Measures include policy development, training, development, and research initiatives to identify the underlying causes.'[48] This puts a puzzling gloss on many real working situations around the globe, and is an assertion with which a number of women's organizations would find it difficult to agree. In fact, the ILO itself concedes that: 'Within both formal and informal mining, women have historically sustained the worst of industry impacts. They are regularly penalised for their gender: consigned to dirtier and more dangerous jobs.'[49] They are also often sexually exploited as prostitutes or 'company wives' and slotted into other pre-designated roles as sustainers of, or handmaidens to, the needs of men.[50] Inevitably, their low social status in many places means they are consigned to the most dangerous tasks. In a broad analysis, the Indian organization mines, minerals and People (mmP) points out that it is the

shift from traditional economies where women had a relatively better control over their bodies and natural resources ... to a life in mining, where they are pitted against prohibitory labour conditions, vagaries of the markets, and lack of any alternatives, that

brings in an entire change in their livelihoods and social life ...
Where Indian women [earlier] formed 30–40% of the workforce
in mining, [this has] been reduced to less than 7% and, in the
coal sector alone, to 4.05%. Schemes like VRS [Voluntary Retire-
ment Schemes] – the golden handshake – have proved a death
knell to women. Women are the pariahs of the large scale mines
... [They] eke out their livelihood by scavenging on the tailings
and wastes dumps, often illegally, and are constantly harassed by
company guards, local mafia or police. They are at the mercy of
local traders for selling their ores. As they are occupied in 'illegal'
mining activities, any accidents like mine collapse where they
are killed or disabled, are most often hushed up by the families
themselves for fear of police action or the company's wrath.'[51]

But this formidable roll-call of indictments against structural gender bias in mining should not lead us to underestimate
women's resilience and their gradually increasing autonomy,
even though current gains seem to be fragile and scattered.
J. J. Hinton points out, in her study of small-scale mining:

The women within these communities are also heterogeneous
and unique; however, they tend to be engaged in specific roles
throughout the world. Typically, they are labourers (e.g. panners,
ore carriers and processors), providers of goods and services
(e.g. cooks, shopkeepers) and are often solely responsible for
domestic chores. Women's responsibilities in mineral processing activities range from crushing, grinding, sieving, washing
and panning, to amalgamation and amalgam decomposition in
the case of gold mining.

Nevertheless, Hinton says,

Less commonly, women are concession owners, mine operators,
dealers and buying agents, and equipment owners. In many
locales, women function in multiple capacities. For instance,

a woman working as a panner may also obtain income as a sex trade worker and a cook. Despite the diverse and important roles undertaken by women in artisanal mining, limited reliable information is available on this topic.[52]

Box 4.2 Women demand inclusion

- We reject the mining operations of national and trans-national corporations that destroy our lands, fragment our societies, displace our communities, perpetrate violence and conflict and influence the legal and policy frameworks in all our countries in order to gain access to the mineral resources. Therefore, from our gender perspective, we believe in harnessing our own resources and demand the withdrawal of these companies where demanded by communities, and that governments promote public sector or community/workers' ownership of mining.

- We oppose the retrenchment and marginalisation of women mine workers and demand their inclusion in the formal and organised sector and demand that they be protected by legislative, executive and judicial norms and safeguards in order to promote the full exercise of their rights to dignity of life, incomes and healthy work environment.

- We demand the recognition of artisanal, traditional and community mining where women play an important part, and that governments provide economic support, development facilities, technology interface, safety measures and market linkages to improve the condition of the women miners and their environment.

- We state that the mining industry is as legally and socially

---

Blood, toil and tears

responsible as our governments are for the child labour directly or indirectly working in the mining sector and demand that they immediately abolish child labour while providing sustainable alternative incomes for their families and education opportunities for the children.

- Mining is an unsustainable industry and does not lead to economic and social well being of people. It forces a situation of unfair trade, economics, health and social relationships.

- Privatisation and liberalisation have completely marginalised women in the mining industry by large scale retrenchment and denial of employment facilities to women. These processes are aggressively being implemented in almost all our countries.

- Women in mining pay the highest price of human degradation for the extraction and enjoyment of minerals and metals by the world. The valuation of the world's minerals does not take into account these invisible human costs and subsidies, especially that women and children pay. Most women in mining communities are forced into illegal mining activities due to displacement, loss of access to natural resources and for lack of proper livelihood options when land based economies shift to mining economies.

- Mining has not only marginalised women in the industry but also destroyed all other livelihood opportunities on which women have been dependent with respect to traditional land, forests and water based occupations. Thereby, it has led to the reduction in the social and economic status of women, especially indigenous women, as a result of forced transition from land based traditional systems to mining based economies.

- The mining industry is perpetrating prejudices that women cannot handle technology and that they have to be largely confined to the unskilled labour.
- Mining has had serious impacts on women workers' health and has caused irrevocable illnesses like silicosis, tuberculosis, asbestosis, chronic, debilitating, terminal and reproductive health problems which are deliberately suppressed by the industry, ignored and neglected by our governments.
- Women mine workers are exposed to high levels of pollution, contamination and toxic substances at the work place and are especially employed in the more hazardous and polluting sections of the mining activities like processing plants and milling units.[53]

Catching them young

Sending very young people into mines and quarries is condemned as among the 'worst' forms of child labour by the ILO, many trade unions and the industry body, the International Council on Mining and Metals (ICMM). This is not surprising since, as well as evincing humanitarian motives, most of these organizations don't want young people to displace organized adult labour, thereby posing threats to minimum wage levels and hard-won social benefits. Generally, a working child is defined as below fourteen years, regardless of their actual intellectual and physical maturity. In Mongolia alone in 2003, of the 100,000 people labouring in informal gold mines, between 10 and 15 per cent were believed to be children.[54] This author has seen a Filipino boy as young as thirteen snaking his way into a hillside adit (horizontal tunnel), barely half a metre high, to scrape out handfuls of gold ore and load them on to a tiny cart. At one

85

Indian bauxite pit, owned by the FTSE ('Footsie') 100 UK company Vedanta Resources, in 2006 I found a seven- or eight-year-old child picking up rocks by hand to deliver to his labouring father. In 2006 Brazil's Social Observatory performed an undercover investigation into conditions for a community dependent on talc mining at the eponymous Minas Talco. It discovered some twenty children from five to seventeen years old, using wheelbarrows to haul out unprocessed rocks, each weighing roughly 18 kilos. The young people went to school in the morning, entering the mines during the afternoon; their families were paid on average less than US$4 a day. On processing, the talc was sold to various manufacturers, including Britain's Imperial Chemical Industries (ICI).[55]

It is common sense to distinguish the highly dangerous exploitation of youngsters hauling coal from deep Colombian pits (say) and the almost 'playful' activity of girls and boys collecting stones in an open-air environment, eager to assist their elders. The former is clearly unacceptable; the latter arguably less so. In general, the risks young people run vary in degree rather than substance. Their vulnerability to lung disorders, injuries and stunted growth is measurably greater than for fully matured adults. The more dangerous the tasks to which they are consigned (especially in any sub-surface digging or carrying), the less visible they will be, and thus the more reduced their capacity to empower themselves in a meaningful way. Does this mean we should characterize all young people in the minerals sector as 'slaves' or as mercilessly exploited? Many agencies addressing the issue recognize that there is no instant solution to 'the problem', since child labour is customarily a response to familial impoverishment; you may take the children out of the mine, but it is far more difficult to abstract mining from the community. The ILO claims that its sponsored schemes in Mongolia, as well as Tanzania, Niger and the Andean countries of South America, have shown that the best way to assist child miners is to work with the children's own communities ... Mining and quarrying communities have been helped to organize cooperatives and improve productivity by acquiring machinery, thus eliminating or reducing the need for child labour. They have also been assisted in obtaining legal protection and developing essential services such as health clinics, schools and sanitation systems ... [W]hile difficult, the problem of child mining and quarrying is not only manageable – it can be solved.[56]

In contrast, efforts to reduce the exploitation of hundreds of thousands of small people who toil alongside their families serving South Asia's building sectors have so far largely failed as they come up against a skein of political self-interests at local and regional levels (see Chapter 5). Blaming parents for permitting their offspring to be abused is not a valid response. They may themselves be entrapped by the bonded labour system, fated to early disability or death, and are frequently paid wages that barely keep them above subsistence level.

Certainly, banning child workers from specific sectors could secure them some respite. Until recently, because of their dexterity and small fingers, children were widely enlisted in India's diamond cutting and polishing shops (*hiravalas*). Stung by accusations of being directly complicit in this exploitation, Anglo De Beers and Rio Tinto – major foreign purchasers of Indian polished diamonds – have taken steps to restrict under-age employment in the sector. Now the *hiravalas* usually 'take in mostly migrant labourers between the ages of 18 and 25'. Recruited from surrounding rural areas, these young men are still 'hired under extreme work conditions – dark ill ventilated rooms, [and paid] highly degrading, poor wages'.[57] The age of those exploited may have risen, but the nature of the daily grind has little improved.

Blood, toil and tears

Small in scale, but big in problems

The spectrum that stretches between trade-union-organized mine labour at one end, and those who scrabble through water-logged mud sinks for a few grains of gold or specks of cobalt at the other, seems vast. Will never the twain meet? In fact, they often have done and will continue to do so. Although officially called a *garimpeiro* (small miner) in Brazil, you may be employed only at certain times of the year, relying on farming for the remainder. You might also find yourself part of an intricate, sometimes ruthless, web of buyers and entrepreneurs.[58] In the late 1980s Anglo American was, at one and the same time, condemning Brazilian small-scale miners for being environmental despoilers, while employing some of them to trace deposits it could then test-drill. Thousands of 'wildcat' Brazilians, scrambling over cassiterite deposits on the Surucusis plateau, marketed their output to middlemen who then sold it to Paranapanema, the country's leading tin producer.[59] When a British ecological group exposed Rio Tinto in the early nineties for its gold prospecting in an Ecuadorian national park, the company cancelled its leases and sacked its Ecuadorian manager, claiming not to be aware it was operating in a protected forest. But it had already sponsored a small-scale mining cooperative in the same national park. In 1995, I travelled along Guyana's Mazaruni river to investigate the activities of diamond prospectors who vacuumed up large gobbets of the river bed, destroying the banks and creating treacherous islands amid the fast-flowing currents. The resourceful Guyanan who accompanied me was vehemently opposed to the practice. On my return to the UK, however, I was reliably informed that this brave soul himself owned a number of diamond dredges, working them in his spare time. Igorot (indigenous) gold panners in the Cordillera region of the Philippines have been allowed to practise small-scale extraction from land owned by the Benguet mining corporation. But, lacking the capital to set up their own mills, they sell their caches in a raw form to the company, earning perhaps a third of what the gold is really worth. Elsewhere in the country, others are poring over prospects, damned as illegal by government and companies alike. During October 2006, Indonesian police arrested forty-three citizens of West Papua when they attempted to extract gold from wastes piling out from Freeport-Rio Tinto's massive Grasberg mine. This wasn't the first time such arrests had occurred, and some miners have been killed for their pains. This conflict bore the hallmarks of a classic clash between poor farmers and two of the world's biggest mining companies. In reality, the police collected a lucrative pay-off from the intruders, while official mine staff turned an unseeing eye on the corruption.

Despite such bewildering contradictions, and the fact that thousands of people may be engaged in extracting ores from just one hillside or along a single river during gold and diamond 'rushes', all these activities are now officially called ASM (Artisanal and Small-scale Mining). This classification does have two potential virtues. It legitimizes 'illegal' operations, triggered by displacement from farming (sometimes the result of a mining company's own legalized land invasion). And it opens the way for officially funded technical assistance, which can diminish dependence on antiquated and dangerous equipment. Any scheme to mitigate the use of mercury in gold amalgamation (a practice that gives rise to extremely potent methyl mercury emissions) must be welcomed. Not so long ago, the minerals industry was spreading a mixture of fact and propaganda to support its contention that ASM was environmentally destructive; skimmed off the best deposits before they could be responsibly extracted; and stole profits from governments when output was smuggled from the country into the arms of middlemen and foreign traders. Several governments proved only too eager to send their armies into the field to clear away the small miners, sometimes leaving several dead behind. Often this aggression was justified as protecting indigenous settlements from alien invasion – even though the local people were themselves digging for gold and other minerals.

We are now led to believe that these bad old days have been firmly put behind us. One of the key tools in this new, socially responsible, armoury is the Kimberley Process, designed to warrant 'clean', as opposed to 'conflict' (or 'blood'), diamonds, in Africa and Latin America. More recent initiatives include the proposed certification of gold, both to wipe out the use of mercury and 'regulate' the irresponsible use of cyanide. As I point out in Chapter 8, however, there is considerable doubt that these short-term strategies will achieve their avowed objectives.

For whatever else the World Bank may be faulted, it has laudably tried to address the ambivalent role of small miners, accused of instigating destructive practices on the one hand, while pitied as casualties of neocolonial politics and mercenary avarice on the other. The bank launched CASM, the Communities and Small Scale Mining initiative, in 2001. Rightly, this organization points out that small-scale mining practices are 'largely a poverty driven activity ... in some of the world's poorest regions [which], if tapped, ... [have] potential to contribute significantly to social and economic development ... The challenge facing the civil society, large-scale mining companies, and governments is to harness ASM as an activity that can contribute responsibly towards the achievement of development objectives.'[60]

The aim is laudable, but its underlying intent may be strongly questioned. Ultimately, the informal is to be merged into the formal under the aegis of governments and multilateral institutions. The strategy risks marginalizing, or even denying, a community's right to ownership of its own subsoil resources and jeopardizing just settlement of its land claims. As recent events in Bolivia (see Box 4.3) have tragically demonstrated, unless these dual claims are legally recognized from the outset, even the most carefully designed programme to bring independent mineworkers into the mainstream is doomed to fail.

Box 4.3 Forced divisions

In late 2006, Bolivian small-scale mineworkers' cooperatives clashed violently with employees of the state mining company Comsur. During one particularly bloody confrontation several lost their lives. Yet both parties were fighting for their survival. The *cooperativos* had taken newly elected president José Morales (himself a former miner) at his word, when he promised that they would be ceded mineral leases. On their part, the state-employed workers were desperately clinging to what was left from the earlier privatization of Comibol, engineered by the disgraced former president 'Goni' Lozado.

During the late nineties, thousands of indigenous, out-of-work mineworkers used their skills to dig out pits in the still highly lucrative tin zone of Huanuni. They had threatened to set up road and rail blocks and occupy the mines, unless the government granted them at least US$600 million in order to revive the sector. The government's intransigence provoked violent protests during which five miners were killed, before Lozado introduced legislation to reform the small mining sector.[61] After a British company, BSG, took over the zone, some workers were re-employed by Comibol; others were left at the mercy of the cold, damp and dangerous pits. In October 2006, sixteen miners were killed, and more than sixty wounded, when members of the cooperatives attempted to take over deposits within Comibol's lease area. The state miners had themselves set up a highway blockade at Huanuni in late September, demanding more jobs at the mine.

Blood, toil and tears

Who was to blame? Comibol accused the *cooperativos* and the UK accountancy firm Grant Thornton, which bought up the debts acquired by RBG when it collapsed in a cloud of ignominy in 2002, found guilty of fraud. Others pointed out that Comibol's workers received lower wages than their adversaries outside the gates.

But these events represented more than mere 'infighting'. At the root of conflict is the neoliberalization of Bolivia's economy in the eighties, which resulted in the evisceration of Comibol and the dismissal of thousands of indigenous miners (including many women and children). They were then left to their own devices – or rather to mining hundreds of scattered deposits, some with their bare hands. Miners on both sides of the divide looked to Morales to resolve a crisis that was not of his own making. At the end of October 2006, he announced that 4,000 'independent' (ASM) miners would be taken on by Comibol.[62]

Forging 'Just Transition'

Examples of collaboration between environmentalists, community activists and mineworkers do not exactly cover the globe; at first sight their respective aims are set too wide apart. After all, trade unionists want job security, and that can hardly be guaranteed if a powerful civil lobby is also calling for mine closure, or demanding a change to government priorities – for example, switching from subsidies for coal to backing solar power. But, in reality, it is often impossible (certainly unwise) to draw neat distinctions between the three constituencies. Those who work in mines also live in neighbouring communities, often suffering the most gravely from any disaster. Likewise, communities that have come to depend on corporate-run facilities or subsidies will fight to keep a project open. This may be so even when operations are clearly detrimental to health, such as at the Doe Run smelter in Peru (see Chapter 6), or in the case of the Ok Tedi mine in Papua New Guinea, where wastes continue to blight an entire ecological subregion. There will have come a point at which initial resistance has given way to seeking the best possible socio-economic deal, and making sure the mining company sticks to it. The earth is strewn with mined-out sites, mercilessly drained of their economic potential, around which residents wait indefinitely for compensation and rehabilitation since they never had the power to negotiate an impacts and benefits agreement with the previous owner, who, in turn, was absolved from banking a post-mine bond.

For a decade now, the Brussels-based ICEM has been cultivating alliances with NGOs. In 1997 it invited the activist umbrella group Partizans to help set an agenda for international militant actions against Rio Tinto. As a result, the mineworkers joined other 'dissident shareholders' at several company annual general meetings between 1997 and 2000. In 1999, the union issued a statement supporting 'sustainable development in ICEM industries [to promote] economic, social and environmental harmony', while recognizing that 'the dynamics between these three imperatives will change over time'. Anticipating the likely attrition on the coal sector from mounting calls to curb global climate change, the ICEM further undertook to 'develop Just Transition policies ... [including] the prevention of environmental dumping, the development of more efficient and clear use of energy and the "sun setting" of obsolete and unwanted products and processes'.[63] Two years later, the ICEM joined civil society organizations in demanding the withdrawal of Canada's Ivanhoe Mines from Burma, stating: '[I]t is the position of the global movements that it is impossible to do business with the Burmese government ... without subsidising forced labour and other

93

human rights violations ... [I]n the case of Ivanhoe's partnership with the military junta, foreign investment is directly propping up the regime.'[64]

These welcome initiatives do not necessarily presage smooth convergence between those struggling against mining at a community level and trade union leaderships. Only a month before the ICEM made its November 1999 commitment to sustainable development, it also pledged to 'increase the consumption of gold', since (or so it claimed) 'each gold mining job directly supports ten people and indirectly creates employment for many more'.[65] Nevertheless, in 2006 the United Steel Workers of America, the largest mineworkers union in North America, established a 'green' alliance with the Sierra Club, one of America's most influential environmental organizations. A little later, Colombia's National Union of Coal Workers (Sintracarbón) inspected the El Cerrejón coal mine in La Guajira province along with several international NGOs and the Wayuu indigenous rights organization Yanama. The union unequivocally declared that:

> The goal of [government and company] policies is to eliminate all sources of employment and the only means that the communities have of supporting themselves. If the UN had created such a category, we might say that these communities are reduced to the conditions of the 'living dead': they do not have the minimal conditions necessary for survival ... If the Cerrejón company has a social responsibility towards these communities, Sintracarbón also has a moral and political responsibility to accompany the communities that are being affected by the expansion of mining ... We invite our union members to take on the communities' problems as our own problems, in the defense of the people of the Guajira.[66]

Amen to that.

Notes

1 International Labour Organization, 'The ILO and Mining', Geneva, <www.ilo.org/public/english/dialogue/sector/sectors/mining/ilo.htm>.

2 The world's largest mine in terms of output is the Grasberg copper-gold operation of Freeport-Rio Tinto in West Papua. According to figures published by the International Copper Study Group (ICSG) in 2000, the mine had 14,000 employees, including contract workers. Of these only 10 per cent (1,400) were 'local' – for which read regional rather than drawn from the indigenous custodians of the vast contract of work (lease) areas. See 'Indonesia's experience: mining and copper 1900–2000', ICSG, Lisbon, 2002, p. 16.

3 Kentuckians Write Against Mountaintop Removal, *Missing Mountains: We Went to the Mountaintop but It wasn't There*, Wind Publications, Nicholasville, KY, 2005, p. 66.

4 Canadian Broadcasting Corporation (CBC), Investigative Unit, 'The McArthur river uranium mine', *48 Hours*, 19 April 2004. The CBC said it had 'uncovered documents that show that Cameco had been worried about [this section of the mine] for months, believing it to have a high potential for a flood. According to these documents, the company planned to have pumps installed but the cave-in beat them to it.'

5 *Independent*, London, 31 July 2002.

6 See ICEM, 'Rio Tinto: behind the façade', 1998 Stakeholders Report, Brussels, 1998, pp. 21–3.

7 Update, International Federation of Chemical, Energy, Mine and General Workers' Unions, Brussels, 7 November 1999.

8 ILO, 'The evolution of employment, working time and training in the mining industry: report for discussion at the tripartite meeting on the evolution of employment, working time and training in the mining industry (TMMI)', Geneva, 2002, p. 14.

9 D. Cevallos, 'Latin America: mining an open pit of disputes', IPS, Mexico City, 9 September 2006.

10 The discussion of occupational diseases in this chapter does not include HIV/Aids. There is no question that mineworkers and their dependants in southern Africa – and elsewhere, such as Indonesia and Burma – are among the worst to suffer among the general population. Migrant labourers are housed in makeshift camps, or single-sex hostels in South Africa, despite an official end to apartheid. The prospect that victims, including wives and other sexual partners, may one day be able to sue their employers for being instrumental in causing this huge attrition is dim indeed. Several mining houses, led by Anglo American, are financing South African programmes aimed at HIV/Aids prevention and treatment using retroviral drugs. Unsurprisingly, one of their major aims (and that of the government) is to ensure that their employees

survive in oder to continue serving the industry: see J. Lamont, 'Gold producers act on HIV', *Financial Times*, London, 24 July 2002. The World Bank in 2002 estimated that up to a third of South Africa's current mine workforce could die from HIV/Aids if drastic steps are not taken. See World Bank/IFC, 'HIV/AIDS and mining', December 2002.

11 'SA mining industry in danger of missing first key health target', *Mining Weekly*, 9 June 2006.

12 See 'Digging deeper', published by PricewaterhouseCoopers, 2003, summarized in *Mining Magazine*, London, April 2006, pp. 22–6.

13 V. Smith, 'Union demands safer coal mines, protests Stickler appointment', Associated Press, 24 October 2006.

14 Ibid.

15 US Department of Labor, 'Coal fatalities for 1900 through 2005'.

16 'Asia energy', *Mining Journal*, 29 September 2006, p. 7.

17 Shaikh Azizur Rahman, 'India's illegal coal mines turn into death pits', *Washington Times*, 26 November 2006.

18 'Mines of death', *Hindu BusinessLine*, 12 September 2006; see also 'Controversy surrounds Indian miner deaths', *Coal Magazine*, London, September/October 2006.

19 R. Dunayevskaya, 'Two pages of history that have shown the way to freedom', from the Raya Dunayevskaya Collection, 23 April 1955, to be found in the Archives of News and Letters, Detroit. Dunayevksaya claimed that more people – including many Jews – died from conditions at the Vorkuta coal mines under Stalin than were murdered in Auschwitz.

20 *Times Educational Supplement*, 3 May 2002.

21 Among the many excellent books describing the lives – and deaths – of coal mineworkers over the centuries, I strongly recommend: William B. Thesig (ed.), *Caverns of Night: Coal, Mines in Art, Literature and Film*, University of South Carolina Press, 2000; and Barbara Freese, *Coal: A Human History*, Perseus Publishing, Cambridge, MA, 2003.

22 Zijun Li, 'Lack of corporate social responsibility behind recent China accidents', China Watch, 12 December 2005.

23 China Labour Bulletin (CLB), Press release no. 10, Hong Kong, November 2005.

24 *Mining Journal*, London, 23 June 2000.

25 *Mining Journal*, London, 29 September 2006.

26 *Xinhuanet*, 20 November 2005.

27 'Deconstructing deadly details from China's coal mine safety statistics', *China Labour Bulletin News*, Flash no. 60, Hong Kong, 6 January 2006.

28 China Labour Bulletin, Press release, 14 November 2006.

29 China Labour Bulletin, Press release, 7 November 2005.

30 One of the least-recognized, but by no means negligible, consequences of digging for coal has been the spontaneous ignition of underground and surface seams in eastern India and parts of South Africa. These cause scores of fires that continue raging to this day, emitting an incalculable amount of CO_2 gases and particulates. Despite efforts by various agencies, including the World Bank, no technology has yet been discovered to quell them.

31 See 'Rotterdam treaty killed by asbestos disease', Press statement by BWI and IBAS, Geneva, 13 October 2006.

32 R. Moody, *The Risks We Run: Mining, Communities and Political Risk Insurance*, International Books, 2005, pp. 54–6.

33 See 'Corporate culpability: Cape and Gencor pay compensation to asbestos disease victims', Press release, John Pickering & Co. Solicitors (UK), 27 June 2003.

34 'WR Grace must pay asbestos clean-up bill', Environment News Service, 11 October 2006.

35 For a graphic personal history of working at the Libby mine, see D. Dimokopoulos, *Exposed*, Life Rattle Press, Toronto, 2006.

36 ILO, 'Facts on safety at work', Geneva, 2005.

37 See 'Gold Fields, Harmony downplay killer TB reports', *Mineweb*, 20 September 2006.

38 'South African miners sue Anglo American for silicosis', PlanetArk (Reuters), 24 August 2004.

39 'SA mining industry in danger of missing first key health target', *Mining Weekly*, June 2006.

40 'Deadly dust: the silicosis epidemic among Guangdong jewellery workers and the defects of China's occupational illnesses prevention and compensation system', China Labour Bulletin, CLB Research Series no. 1, December 2005.

41 B. Sharples, 'After the Lihir landslide', *Mining News*, Australia, 14 October 2005.

42 Ibid.

43 *Guardian*, 27 February 2000.

44 *Financial Times*, 12 February 2000.

45 K. Robinson, 'A bitter harvest', *New Internationalist*, Oxford, March 1999.

46 ILO, 'The evolution of employment', p. 14.

47 *Guardian*, 20 February 2003, p. 19.

48 ILO, 'The evolution of employment', p. 15.

49 Ibid.

50 See Robinson, 'A bitter harvest'.

51 'Labour and women in mining', Background paper by mines, minerals and People (mmP) for the Indian Women and Mining

seminar, Delhi, April 2003, <www.minesandcommunities.org/Mineral/women4.htm>.

52 J. Hinton and M. Vega et al., 'Women and artisanal mining: gender roles and the road ahead', in G. Hilson, *The Socio-economic Impacts of Artisanal and Small-scale Mining in Developing Countries*, A. A. Balkema, Netherlands, 2003, p. 2.

53 Taken from the Declaration of the International Women and Mining Conference, Visakhapatnam, India, 1–9 October 2004, in <mmP (India), <www.mmPindia.org/womenmining.htm>.

54 Union Network International, 'World Day Against Child Labour 2005: digging for survival – the harsh reality of child mining worldwide', 9 June 2005.

55 K. Goodwin, 'Child labour used in Brazilian mines that supply ICI plants', *Independent*, 7 March 2006.

56 See ILO, 'Gold rush in Mongolia: when shepherds become "ninjas"', ILO, Geneva, 2 September 2005.

57 'Labour and women in mining'.

58 G. MacMillan, *At the End of the Rainbow?: Gold, Land and People in the Brazilian Amazon*, Earthscan, London, 1995.

59 Ibid., p. 46.

60 CASM (2006), 'ASM: from threat to opportunity', World Bank, Washington, DC.

61 D. Bocangel, 'Small-scale mining in Bolivia: National Study for Mining, Minerals and Sustainable Development project', Paper 71, MMSD, London, August 2001, p. 71.

62 D. Keane, 'Bolivian mining groups declare truce', Associated Press, 6 October 2006; Dan Keane, 'Morales fires 2 Bolivia mining officials', Associated Press, 7 October 2006. See also 'Bolivian mining reforms delayed', *Mining Journal*, 3 November 2007.

63 ICEM Update, no. 66/1999, 5 November 1999.

64 ICEM Update, no. 39/2001, 15 June 2001.

65 ICEM Update no. 62/1999.

66 'Report by the international delegation – Yanama – SINTRA-CARBÓN to the SINTRACARBÓN plenary: impact of the Cerrejón mine expansion on the communities in the mining area', Colombia, 7 November 2006.

5 | The destruction of construction

Among the hardest places for human survival are those where rocks, comprising the bulkiest single category of materials extracted from our planet, are blasted, drilled, chipped, crushed and sieved. Millions of tonnes of aggregates get moved every day to provide the foundation for highways, ports, railways and dams. Gravels mixed with cement (a combination of sand, lime, gypsum and chemicals) underpin the fabric of villages, towns and cities. Clays are shaped, baked and turned into bricks, then glued together with cement to create our homes, factories, museums and military bases. Sandstone may be crafted into tiles, slabs (for tables, benches, gravestones), building strips, decorative pebbles and bricks. Kaolin (china clay) goes into paint, distemper, paper and pharmaceuticals, as well as crockery. Silica ends up as glass for windows, bottles for the table and in the computers sitting on many of our desks.

The market for construction materials has never been stronger. China, the world's biggest producer and consumer of cement, churns out more than 30 billion tonnes of it a year. Sandstone production from the Indian state of Rajasthan doubled between 1995 and 2000 (from 4,106 to 8,369 million tonnes), meeting an estimated 10 per cent of global demand.[1] Global demand is accelerating, and not just due to rising consumer expectations of 'quality' housing and ever more roads; it's also the inevitable consequence of devastation caused by climate change and war. One project, the Iraqi government's 'Rebuild Iraq 2007', is worth at least 100 billion dollars to contractors fortunate enough to make a killing, and such high returns are not exceptional. Hanson, the Anglo-American conglomerate that is one of the world's leading brick manufacturers, enjoys assets of around 7 billion dollars. Cement producer Lafarge made just under 5 billion euros' worth of sales in the first half of 2006 alone.

Owing to their weight and size, big stones usually don't travel far. The main exceptions are certain grades of sandstone, granite, slate, limestone, quartzite and marble, know collectively as 'natural' or 'dimension' stone. Marble is exported all over the globe, primarily from Italy, China and India – where workers are lowered by cradles into deep and precarious pits. High-quality cement also crosses borders with ease. Until recently Asian and African manufacturers served mainly local requirements, but a new cohort of multinational cement suppliers has emerged over the past ten years, consolidating control through mergers and acquisitions and exporting widely outside their own domains. Cimenterie Nationale of France, for example, accesses markets in Syria and Iraq, North Africa, the USA and Canada. A South–South trade is also burgeoning: some Indian manufacturers sell their output to the United Arab Emirates.[2]

Most of us have yet to recognize the extent and nature of this global profit-taking. Pave your driveway with help from the UK's RMC (eponymous supplier of ready-mixed concrete) and you may well fancy you are 'buying British': in fact the company was acquired by Cemex of Mexico in 2004. When Lafarge took over Blue Circle (virtually a UK household name) in 2001, it not only ended up in French hands but instantly propelled Lafarge to the top of the cement premiership.[3] Buy 'Gujarat Ambuja' cement in India and, in reality, you're helping line the pockets of the Schmidheiny family of Switzerland. Their Holcim conglomerate snapped up the company for US$800 million in 2005, marking the costliest foreign takeover of any Indian domestic company until that date.[4]

Some big companies, normally identified only for their metals interests, have also consolidated ownership in construction raw materials; it's profitable and saves costs in building their own offices, mine approach roads, loading bays and shafts. The world's fourth-biggest mining conglomerate, Anglo American, holds important limestone and rock interests, as well as controlling Tarmac, the UK's largest supplier of aggregates, asphalt and concrete blocks. Japan's premier trading conglomerate, Mitsubishi – a highly significant investor in ferrous and non-ferrous mining – sells aggregates, cement and ceramic tiles in the USA.

These world players naturally benefit from the lower cost of raw materials, fuel and labour available in the South, especially in Asia. They have a clear and well-thought-out strategy of amalgamation with smaller, regionally based companies, typified by Cemex of Mexico's recent bids for stakes in Philippine companies, and Hanson's penetration of Malaysia (where it boasts of 'transforming' the country's urban skyline through supplies of aggregates and asphalt).

Yet, on the ground, the two Asia-Pacific countries with the biggest potential for 'growth' in construction, China and India, still cling to elementary methods of extraction, milling and processing, although mechanization is gradually increasing. Operations centre on small pits and makeshift kilns in thousands of locations where labourers toil under derisory 'contracts' (often none at all), bound to often quasi-criminal middlemen. Commonly dubbed a 'mafia' in India, these entrepreneurs are not a peculiarly Asian breed. As two UK researchers concluded in 2004: 'It is not Polish bricklayers who drag UK construction down – rather, the sector's brutish nature makes it rely, for much of its existence, upon the almost feudal practice of day labouring.'[5]

'Broken – just like the stone we break'

Though Turkey, Iran, Brazil and South Africa are among the rising exporters of natural stone[6] by far the dominant producers are India and China. The world's most populous state has more quarries than its neighbour, but also imports Indian stones before 'dressing' and re-exporting them, so trade statistics can be misleading. Regrettably there is a dearth of detail on working conditions in Chinese mines in general and quarries in particular. But, according to government statistics, 75 per cent of all occupational disease in the country is due to pneumoconiosis,[7] of which the primary causes are dust in coal mines, silica inhalation (most acute during sand-blasting) and emissions from cement kilns.[8]

It's impossible to calculate exactly how many people toil by the sweat of their brows to supply the bedrock of our infrastructures and beautify our shelters. One source puts the global figure of direct employees in the construction industry at 110 million.[9] This is inevitably a guesstimate and probably represents only half the true number. Consider that there are as many as 6,000 types of natural stone being worked on any day, and that 11 million tonnes were imported into the European Union alone in 2002.[10] It requires an awful lot of fingers – many of them tiny – to deliver such variety and tonnage.

A large proportion of the total workforce is peripatetic, seasonal or recruited locally for a specific project – a bypass, bridge or block of flats. Hundreds of thousands of labourers are female and under fourteen years of age; unregistered because they have been illegally recruited. Conditions for construction employees, wherever they work around the world, are always potentially hazardous, as recognized by key ILO Conventions.[11] In theory these standards are incorporated into national legislation by virtually all those states where violations are most common. The rules are consistently breached, however – and not just in South Asia. A 2005 survey of one site in Zambia found 'a number of women with children strapped to their backs, crushing the stones without any protective clothing'.[12]

Undoubtedly the most insidious impacts derive from mine

owners' use of 'bonded labour', a system synonymous with slavery. It makes 'owing one's soul to the company store' – that immortal jingle coined by country and western singer Merle Travis, to reflect his family's experience in the Kentucky coal mines of the 1930s – seem a mild irritant in comparison.[13]

Bonded labour condemns millions of women and children to working off debts, and the interest accrued on them, by a male head of the family, sometimes for several generations. The system is most prevalent in India, and particularly damaging to women, despite the government's ratification, more than fifty years ago, of ILO Convention no. 29 against Forced Labour, and promulgating its own Bonded Labour System (Abolition) Act in 1976. The latter purportedly frees all bonded labourers and guarantees total liquidation of their debts, but examples of successful enforcement are few and far between. It would be a grave mistake to dismiss widespread contraventions of the rules as merely capricious, or blame them solely on site foremen and local bosses. Burma's forced labour, ubiquitous in quarries, gem mines and on road and rail construction projects, is press-ganged by the military regime itself.

In India and Pakistan the abuse of workers is often systemic, rooted in discrimination and casteism, endorsed by powerful political figures at local and state level. The bigger the potential profits in delivery from mine to manufacture, the more lucrative will be the corrupt rake-offs. A 2005 study judges that half a million Indian workers are employed in the natural stone industry in Rajasthan alone.[14] Examining conditions in one village, Budhpura, the authors comment: 'Quarry owners are generally not involved in retail selling, processing or exporting of sandstone ... [The] buyers are generally traders with collection centres or warehouses in Kota, Jaipur or in Delhi ... sell[ing] crude or roughly trimmed sandstone to domestic and international customers.'[15] The majority of stonecutters in the district belong to so-called

Scheduled Castes (sub-castes or Dalits, who used to be derisorily classified as 'untouchables' or Harijans). Decision-making lies entirely in the hands of the dominant upper castes, however, who, in the village elections of February 2005, won all the seats, with the vital posts of village president and director (head of the village parliament) going to quarry owners.[16] Although discrimination against Scheduled Castes is expressly forbidden under Article 15 of the Indian Constitution, industrial encroachment has forced many of them to sell land to the government's Revenue Department. Their farms and plots are then leased out for quarrying and – in an exiguous inversion of natural justice – the farmers end up working in quarries as labourers themselves or as petty contractors. The registered population of Budhpura is some 4,400 people, but stone pits in the district as a whole employ around 25,000 people, most of them from Scheduled Tribes who have migrated from as far afield as Jharkhand to the east, and Tamil Nadu in India's far south.[17]

'This transformation of land use at Budhpura has resulted in an almost 50 per cent reduction in irrigated land; meanwhile the price of an acre of arable land in the quarry area has risen well beyond the regional average.'[18] Agriculture therefore no longer provides sustainable livelihoods for many who were formerly dependent on the soil, or they have been forced to substitute mustard for thirstier rice varieties or wheat, resulting in lower incomes.[19] Even so, '[t]hey are not able to reap a good harvest even when the rainfall is above average. The layers of quarry dust that settle on the leaves stall the growth and flowering of the crops. The water level of wells and ponds in the area has dropped drastically due to the frequent deepening of quarry pits around the village' – rendering them ideal breeding grounds for malarial mosquitoes.[20] Wages have fallen too – by up to 15 per cent of late, despite the increase in sandstone exports. Hired out to subcontractors, the labour squads never work directly under the quarry owner. '[They] cannot claim any medical expenses, insurance cover, earned holidays or any other compensation in the event of accident or death. No records are maintained ... making it difficult for them to avail or claim compensation or any other benefits accrued on the quarrying company or from the government.'[21] Basic sanitation and adequate fresh water are non-existent in the quarry areas. Instead, most residents use quarry water for washing clothes and bathing and women walk up to 2 kilometres for drinking water. Workers' houses do not have a legal electricity connection, with the result that illegal (and dangerous) connections are rampant.[22]

As for environmental despoliation:

In the Budhpura quarries ... the amount of usable stone has never been more than 25% of all the material upturned ... There is a considerable amount of waste generated from trimming of edges of the slabs. Broken pieces, irregular and odd shaped blocks, lie scattered in the quarrying areas as well as in processing units. The quarrying waste is dumped in forest areas as well as on land belonging to the revenue department, generally without permission, destroying the natural vegetation and ecology of the area. There are many waste dumps of 5–20 metres in height around the Budhpura quarrying sites ...[23]

If a quarry proves no longer profitable, 'the owner abandons it ... to move on to new areas ... There is no specific legislation in India which covers the requirements for environmental protection during the closure of a mine.'[24]

Many observers (including this author) can testify that basic safeguards, mandatory for quarry workers in the North, are almost invariably not applied to stone-breakers in South Asia. Occasionally they will wear helmets, sometimes boots, but only exceptionally are they provided with breathing masks, gloves and protective clothing. Mine owners may claim to offer all these items, blaming their workers for not requesting them; in practice the equipment rarely exists. In any case, day labourers will rarely ask for protective gear, either because it's cumbersome to wear in the heat, or they fear being sacked as potential troublemakers. Consequently, they always face the dangers of rock falls, blasting and of contracting serious occupational diseases, specifically silicosis, pneumoconiosis, bronchitis and tuberculosis. They take their meals in or around the pits, have to urinate and defecate behind trees (especially humiliating for women) and, if seriously injured, must customarily travel miles before they reach a hospital. Accident compensation, when there is any, is negligible, while pensions, healthcare or the right to organize a union are consistently denied.

But the attrition doesn't stop (or even start) at the mining site. It is also grounded in a fundamental failure – shared by regulatory regimes and public perception alike – to distinguish the digging up of rocks from other forms of mining, such as open-pit coal, iron, bauxite or diamond extraction, where workers face compatible risks. By operating a 'quarry', bosses in India can safely ignore the environmental and workplace standards legally imposed on other mining operations. The duty of inspecting stone mines resides with state, not central, government; trained officers from the Indian Bureau of Mines and Directorate General of Mine Safety (DGMS) have no authority to control what goes on. Pits with a design output below a certain tonnage do not require environmental impact assessments, so most quarries will be exempt. Nevertheless, owners will often apply for several leases under different names, effectively ending up with plots that extend to five or more hectares.

Managers of metallic mines, too, wash their hands of responsibility to workers by depending on the pernicious contract labour system. The author visited several such Indian operations between 2000 and 2006. One iron mine in Orissa was officially operated by the state mining company in joint venture with UK's Rio Tinto. In practice the companies bought ore from a haulage firm employing twenty or so local men and youths. Under the lee of a crumbling, almost vertical cliff, they smashed rocks by sledgehammer, sorting and pitching them into trucks with their bare hands. The reward was the national minimum wage of roughly one dollar for a ten-hour day, but only provided that they collectively filled a 10-tonne truck. A high-ranking Indian team which inspected iron ore and granite mines, in the Bellary district of Karnataka in April 2005, was appalled to discover around 200,000 (*sic*) girls and boys, from five years up, 'working in the most hazardous conditions and leading a "pits" of existence between survival and death'. The youngsters not only had to break and carry stones, but were also 'collecting kerosene from mine tailings and in the washeries, handling toxic wastes with their bare hands'.[25] From interviews with contractors, mine owners, workers and local media, the team surmised that 'there may be large black market transactions with exporters from China, Korea and other countries and ... traders within the country'.[26] It concluded that '[t]he entire chain of mining operators including central and state governments, all the private, public and illegal mine owners in the district, the traders, buyers, national and multinational companies connected to iron ore mining and processing, contractors and others involved in the mine extraction, processing and marketing, are equally responsible for the existence of child labour'.[27]

Gradually – but far too sluggishly – the health predicament of South Asian and Chinese stone-breakers is being addressed. Some Indian state governments now have legislation on their books designed to tackle silicosis as an occupational disease. Today, the diagnosis of pneumoconiosis officially covers silicosis, as well as asbestosis and any disease accompanied by pulmonary tuberculosis (TB). Unfortunately, enforcement of the law is weak at best, while patchy implementation has led to further insecurity. After agitation by residents of Delhi's Lal Kuan area in 1992, several silica-stone quarries were closed by order of the Indian Supreme Court. This left the mainly tribal workers stranded and bereft of compensation, since they could not prove a link between their silicosis and previous employment. All too often, driven by expediency, a doctor will wrongly identify TB as the sole culprit, even though it is often a direct result of silicosis, displaying similar symptoms. According to Dr T. K. Joshi of the Department of Occupational and Environmental Medicine at the Maulana Azad Medical College in Delhi, silica is

> perhaps the most toxic particulate matter that can destroy human life ... Crystalline silica dust causes a fibrogenic reaction in the lungs. The ability to breathe is compromised. Blood vessels get obstructed and you could have heart failure. It also has the unique ability to destroy macrophages in the lungs. Therefore, immunity is compromised ... In crowded places like India, it is impossible not to be exposed to tubercule bacilli. Those who have silicosis will also get TB, but the difference is that TB can be cured whereas silicosis is irreversible.[28]

The left-wing Indian news weekly *Frontline* in 2005 graphically depicted the consequences for one laid-off stone-crusher in the Shankargarh block of Allahabad district, Uttar Pradesh:

> Ram Jiyawan crawls to the door of his hovel in Quarry No. 5 to meet this correspondent. After 30 years of breaking silica stone, crushing it, breathing it in as dust and coughing it out as disease, Jiyawan has been left too ill even to walk upright, and too breathless to tell his story. He has been taking treatment for tuberculosis (TB) for the last year and a half, but the medicines do not work.

> In Jiyawan's village of 150 families, 'each man, woman and

many of the children work in silica or stone quarries'. One woman, Meera, told the magazine: 'We're broken; just like the stone we break. Medicine keeps you alive. But there's a fine choice to be made between food and medicine. A week's dose costs Rs.130–150 [nearly US$4]; our daily wages are Rs.40–45 [around US$1].' None of the estimated 25,000 quarry workers in Shankargarh block had even heard of silicosis. All they know is that every third person among them is diagnosed with TB, and that the average life span of a worker is forty years. People have begun to refer to the disease as 'shankargarh-wali TB' (the TB of Shankargarh).[29]

Bricks in the wall

The scouring out of clay, fashioning it with water and subsequent baking into pots or bricks attracts little critical attention. Few industrial pursuits seem less noxious, more utilitarian and free of adverse environmental consequences. Eco-sensitive travellers through South Asia are delighted to chance upon a railway tea stall offering tiny earthenware cups, since these were almost completely usurped by plastic during the 1990s. If the empty vessels aren't carried home as a trophy, they will be thrown upon the ground – sent 'earth to earth' as the apparent epitome of recycling. In fact, the stallholder will usually have an ample supply of plastic cups at hand for his more sophisticated customers; and clay mining is far from innocent of causing damage to water supplies and spreading silica dust. In early 2005, several thousand villagers near Trivandrum, the capital of the Indian state of Kerala, indicted seven local clay mining outfits, before the state's Human Rights Commission, for ruthlessly depleting their water supplies, causing the drying-up of many wells.[30]

By far the biggest market for clays is the brick-making industry, recently identified by another human rights commission in Pakistan as exploiting 'the most deprived section of society'.[31]

The commission found no fewer than three hundred brick kilns in Multan City alone, only ninety-eight of which were registered with the Labour Department. Workers were legally entitled to 2 dollars daily for making a thousand bricks, but claimed never to receive even this derisory amount. An average family (six members including small children) took a whole day to complete the assignment. Rape of women, and the imprisonment of dissident male workers in chains, by kiln owners, were common practice. Although labourers have a constitutional right to establish their own union, no one had ventured to do so. Bonded labour practices were common:

> The [workers] wake up early in the morning irrespective of the season and prepare mud to produce bricks with cold water ... They borrow loans from their kiln owner for marriages of their daughter or sons, which they are not able to pay back throughout their lives, because the interest rate on the loan is so high that the actual loan remains payable while the instalments paid only cover the interest.[32]

A group of brick kiln workers in Lahore recently did dare to organize. Shortly afterwards, one of its leaders was attacked by an armed group of men – and beaten to death in his own courtyard. Shoukat Masih and his family had spent many years opposing the use of bonded labour ('haris' or 'debt slaves') in Punjab's brick kilns. Finally, he helped form a union to file complaints to the government, which were usually ignored. In late 2005 Masih was sold by one brick kiln owner to another for $3,300 without his knowledge or consent. Thereupon he told his story to a local reporter, triggering the attack that felled him. Masih's father is convinced his son had been targeted by a secretive protection racket called 'the SP group', allegedly set up by local kiln owners.[33]

Pakistan human rights activists estimate the country's bonded labour force at around 8 million people (more than 2 per cent of the population). As in India, they are supposedly protected by the authorities should they attempt to flee their intolerable conditions. Many do not even try, resigned to the impossibility of finding safe alternative employment. Thanks to strong ties between kiln owners and local politicians, those who do escape will usually '[be] caught by the police, tortured and sold to another brick kiln owner'.[34]

Nevertheless, a small number succeed (see Box 5.2). Might such still-isolated triumphs one day build into an irresistible movement? Certainly, earlier international campaigns have helped limit the exploitation of Asian children in diamond-cutting shops and carpet factories. But these campaigns depended on the diligent international exposure of the chain of complicity between employers, traders, wholesalers and national and overseas consumers. It might seem high time that those who buy such life-wrecking rocks and bloodstained bricks, as well as the agencies marketing them, were targeted by a similar campaign; whether such a 'chain of custody' could actually function is another issue.

Shifting sands

Within a time frame of millennia, rocks will end up as sand, containing oxidized quantities of key elements in our planet's 'crust'. Silica (silicon dioxide) is found in virtually all sands; both coastal and inland mineral sands include quantities of so-called 'heavy minerals' – titanium, zirconium, radioactive monazite – as well as iron. The grades of metal are low, however, and huge quantities of the raw material must be gouged out to access them: for example, Rio Tinto's titanium concession in Madagascar stretches in a narrow belt for 2,000 hectares up the island's south-eastern coast. This type of extraction is mechanized, often using large floating dredges, and pre-smelt processing is normally performed close by. In contrast, the removal of sand for construction or leisure purposes is carried out on every conceivable scale. Mum and Dad shovel up a few dozen kilos from a neighbouring beach and dump them in the garden to amuse the children. Small contractors employ a bulldozer and a modest fleet of trucks, selling sand to nearby building sites. A big corporation will snatch billions of tonnes of it in any year. The Hanson corporation was accused in 2003 of 'piracy' by California's attorney general for allegedly 'stealing' up to US$60 million worth of sand from San Francisco Bay and artificially lowering the sales price to escape appropriate taxes.[35]

The cumulative effect of all these enterprises is staggering. Yet we still have no consolidated research to highlight how much damage is being done. What few data emerge paint a highly disturbing picture of operations so pervasive, so out of control, that many jurisdictions find it impossible to contain them – even if they really wanted to. The Indonesian islands of Riau host some of the cleanest, most valued sands anywhere. Since the late 1990s they have been coveted by Singapore to feed its expanding construction industry and also to build the foundations for a physical extension of the state itself, pressured by its expanding population. In 2001 Singapore's requirements for Riau sand were estimated at around 1.3 billion tonnes per year, supplied by legal and illegal contractors, some of whom were allegedly linked to the Indonesian navy. The Indonesian Centre for Forestry Studies revealed in 2001 that parts of the seabed surrounding the islands had already been dug to a depth of 12 metres, badly damaging 400,000 hectares and some coral reefs. Declared the centre's director: 'It would take the marine ecosystem at least 30 years to heal.'[36]

It was not until late 2004 that the threat to Riau's sands appeared to lift – ironically when the islands were battered by even greater forces in the shape of the Asia-Pacific tsunami. Finally, international environmentalists began identifying Asian beaches, adjacent wetlands and coral reefs (themselves often blasted to provide lime for cement) as key natural buffers to such a 'perfect storm'. In January 2005 a Tamil Nadu-based chapter of the Indian National Trust for Art and Cultural Heritage declared that, had the Indian government-owned firm, Indian Rare Earths Limited, along with private mineral companies, not earlier removed millions of tonnes of coastal sand, 'many lives would have been saved' from the tsunami.[37] (Adding insult to injury, government scientists visiting Kerala, soon after the horrendous wave struck, gleefully reported that the tsunami had uncovered titanium-bearing deposits, thus making them more accessible to extraction. Incensed local fisherfolk not only demonstrated against further exploitation, but also blamed past mining for causing the disaster.) Six months later, in its Final Report on the impacts of the tsunami, the United Nations Environment Programme (UNEP) also confirmed that sand mining was a significant factor in the ensuing loss of life and habitat. While some estuaries and flatlands in Sri Lanka had failed to prevent waves reaching up to 3 kilometres inland, elsewhere natural dunes had stopped the onslaught just behind the beach line. Furthermore, said UNEP, an increased demand for sand in post-tsunami construction, the chopping down of trees to fuel cement kilns, and relocation of villages to sensitive ecological zones had 'the potential to cause more irreversible damage to Sri Lanka's environment than did the tsunami itself'.[38]

Yet still, an appropriate response to rampant sand extraction continues to elude the world's biggest environmental and development NGOs; it is simply not a priority issue. Instead, the uphill task of making it one mainly falls upon under-resourced organizations responding to the alarm of local and regional communities. One 2005 study by the Kerala NGO Pampa Parirakshana Samithi attributed a recent huge drop in state water availability from three major river basins (by an estimated 4,394 million cubic metres) both to deforestation and sand mining. The river beds formerly acted as 'natural check dams'; however, 'in the absence of sand, no natural retention of water takes place. Sediment deficient flow of "hungry water" picks up more sediment from the stream below the mining site, furthering the degradation.'[39]

Cement: the burning question

It could well be the wonder building material of modern times. Which of us has not benefited in some way from its use? To date there appears to be no substitute for its intrinsic qualities. That said, cement is anything but a pure product, conjured up through some benevolent alchemy. Depending on the quality desired (degree of bulk, flexibility, durability and strength), its basic ingredient of mined limestone will also require the addition of gypsum, quarried shale, clay, marble, iron ore, calcium silicate, dolomite and chlorine. For some brands, high alumina clays – a by-product of bauxite mining – are much sought after. Sulphate-rich rocks go into the manufacture of 'super sulphate' cement. Most worrying of all, in several countries chrysotile asbestos – of which Russia and Canada are the key miners and exporters – is added to increase fire resistance. Despite their being banned in forty states, including throughout the European Union and the USA, India's demand for these carcinogenic fibres is growing by around 9 per cent a year, both for cement and housing (including schools).[40]

Cement mixes are fired together at very high temperatures in kilns fuelled by almost anything that will ignite. The output of this 'miraculous mortar' therefore threatens a triple jeopardy. Mining of limestone (which itself is also burned in kilns) gives rise to vast clouds of silica-laden dust and spoil heaps. Following heavy rains these turn into alkaline lakes that overflow into neighbouring waterways or penetrate underground aquifers, threatening water quality. The raw materials contain toxics (sulphates, sulphides, iron pyrites, nitrogen) which, if not captured in the burning process, will deliver sulphur dioxide to the atmosphere, thus triggering acid rain. Conventional fuels (coal, coke, gas, timber, oil) fed to the kilns are often high in sulphur, nitrogen and heavy metals; they are also a major factor in global climate change.[41]

The world's big cement manufacturers have taken some steps to limit these egregious impacts. Modern plants instal flue gas desulphurization, reduce nitrous oxide output, limit input of high-alkaline materials, and capture some of the particulates to avert potential choking of entire local populations. These measures in themselves do not, however, guarantee a significant lowering of greenhouse gas emissions, nor do they cope with other types of pollution; and they may not be applied in different countries even by the same company. Faith in 'tough' enforcement regimes can also be sorely misplaced. Up to the date of writing no limits on mercury emissions have been applied to US cement plants because the federal Environmental Protection Agency (EPA) 'concluded no reasonably priced controls are available [sic]'.[42] This malfeasance was dramatically exposed in August 2006, when Oregon's Department of Environmental Quality revealed that state-based cement kilns were coughing out more airborne mercury than any other single industrial sector. The Ash Grove cement plant at Durkee was the third-largest source of mercury emissions in the entire country – outstripped only by a California cement plant and Nevada gold mines operated by Newmont Mining.[43] In fact, in 2004 the Durkee kiln had 'vented into the air more than a ton of mercury, hundreds of pounds more than the nation's largest coal-burning power plant, according to federal figures'.[44]

Heading the list of accusations nailed to the industry's cement doors is that companies have done little, or nothing, to reduce their contribution to global warming, estimated at 5 per cent of the total burden. In 1999, shortly after eight metallic mining companies set up the Global Mining Initiative (GMI) (see Chapter 7), ten leading cement producers launched their own Cement Sustainability Initiative under the auspices of the World Business Council for Sustainable Development (WBCSD). The collaboration came as little surprise: Swiss citizen Stephan Schmidheiny, who engineered the founding of the WBCSD seven years earlier, has also derived a sizeable fortune from his interests in cement (see Box 5.1). Just as the GMI delegated framing of its corporate social responsibility agenda to the UK-based International

Box 5.1 An eternity of misdeeds

Stephan Schmidheiny and his brother Thomas are the most prominent members of the Swiss family that founded (through their grandfather Ernst) the cement-asbestos company Eternit and later Holcim, now one of the world's two biggest cement producers. Holcim was controlled up until 2003 by Thomas Schmidheiny. Though giving up the chairmanship that year, he holds on to a directorship and a considerable number of Holcim shares.

Stephan is best known as a 'philanthropist' and founder of the Business (later, World Business) Council for Sustainable Development during the first United Nations World Summit on Sustainable Development (WSSD), held in Rio de Janeiro in 1992. According to some critics, this was a strategy to dislodge the United Nations Center on Transnational Corporations as it moved towards enforceable rules governing the operations of multinational corporations. Schmidheiny also set up AVINA, a charitable foundation which, by 2004, had disbursed some US$291 million for 'sustainable development' partnerships. In 2005 Stephan's personal fortune was estimated by *Forbes* magazine at US$2.8 billion – making him the 210th richest person in the world. True to his new avatar as a doyen of 'sustainability', in 2000 Schmidheiny was also instrumental in establishing the Battelle initiative to 'green' the cement industry.

Ironically, AVINA's largest single tranche of funding goes to projects in Brazil. The irony is that, in 2004, a court in São Paulo indicted Eternit (the Schmidheinys) for causing massive damage to the health of workers in its asbestos operations. The court awarded the aggrieved and their dependants both compensation and the right to adequate medical care.

Eternit's operations span many decades, with a historic liability that stretches around the world – in Europe and South Africa, as well as Latin America. Eight of its former executives were sentenced to a total of twenty-three years' imprisonment in 2005, for putting former employees at risk in Sicily. One of the indicted was Leo Mittelholzer, in charge of the Eternit plant between 1984 and 1986, when the duty of care and corporate responsibility went directly to the Schmidheiny family. Until that year, according to the International Ban Asbestos Secretariat, Mittelholzer was managing director of Siam City Cement, Thailand's second-largest cement company and itself a subsidiary of Holcim.

The huge profits made by Holcim in recent years clearly outweigh any qualms its business peers may nurse about the company's chequered past. In September 2005, the company was anointed a 'leader of industry' by the Dow Jones Sustainable Development Index – primarily for its efforts at mitigating adverse climate change. Of course, not a word was uttered about asbestos.[45]

Institute for Environment and Development (IIED), so the heads of cement handed that task to the Battelle Memorial Institute, a non-profit-making US consultancy. The institute laid down three challenges: 'increasing stakeholder engagement', 'understanding [*sic*] the industry's social contributions' and 'reducing the industry's eco-footprint', in particular its role in hastening negative climate change.

Led by Lafarge, the companies interpreted these behests (they were hardly imperatives) in three broad strokes. They enlarged their social contributions (Lafarge has been building low-cost housing for Indians) and increased pretended 'stakeholder engagement'. But the critical task of 'reducing the industry's eco-footprint' has inevitably proved the most problematic: how to continue making a profit, increase production (especially when this relies on output from newly acquired and less 'responsible' companies) and still bear the expense of cleaning up your act? Fortunately, the solution was already there in the shape of national and local authorities struggling to dispose of a rising tide of industrial, clinical, domestic and agricultural wastes. Cement manufacturers offered to take this avalanche of detritus off government hands – and thereby cut their own costs. Fossil fuels would be phased out and new fuels waved in, all in the name of promoting greener values. As a result, the kilns have opened their hatches to a veritable cocktail of chemicals, biomass, steel slag, medical wastes, animal corpses, fly ash, radioactive substances and – increasingly – worn-out tyres. In Britain today the largest single component of this newer breed of kilns is disused tyres:[46] 40 billion of them ended up on open pyres and inside incinerators in the UK during 2003 alone,[47] significantly adding to the toll of heavy metals, dioxins, furans and persistent organic pollutants spewed into the atmosphere.

Just how did such an astonishingly reckless project get sold to the public in the space of a few years? First, it was necessary to recast the language, transmuting filthy discarded solvents and chemicals into 'substitute Liquid Fuels' ('SLFs')[48] and neutralizing the bad old image of incineration by dubbing it 'co-incineration' fed by these 'alternative fuels'. Next, scientific opinion had to be marshalled in support of the new proposals. This was effected in the UK in 2003 by a government Environment Agency review approving 'the use of Substitute Fuels in Cement and Lime Kilns' – despite no major investigation ever having been carried out into the health of people living around cement kilns already burning toxic wastes.[49]

Finally, it was important to recruit a credible and internationally renowned environmental NGO, prepared to endorse 'alternative fuels' as a bold, constructive step towards mitigating adverse climate change. The coup was struck in 2001 when the Worldwide Fund for Nature (WWF) linked arms with Lafarge in what has, effectively, become a process of certification for the company's plants, based not on site-by-site investigation but primarily on evaluating their global greenhouse gas emissions.

Until three years ago, this three-pronged strategy seemed to be working in favour of the industry, but then the consensus began to crack. In 2003 WWF had failed to speak out against a proposal by its partner, Lafarge, to dig a massive quarry on the Scottish island of Harris, a project that other British environmental groups roundly condemned. At almost the last hour WWF finally joined the chorus of opposition; the plan was thrown out of court in early 2004 (see Box 5.2). Five months later, Germany's Heidelberg Cement and the World Bank proudly launched a programme to showcase the benefits of co-incineration in Indonesia and channel income from the company's 'carbon credits' to poor communities.[50] Shortly before the launch, however, two fisherfolk from one such impoverished community, on Rampa Island in South Kalimantan, were arrested for protesting against the dumping by a Heidelberg subsidiary of masses of waste rock into their bay.

The community's struggle had already lasted two years, with the livelihoods of thousands of people allegedly jeopardized.[51]

In 2005, India's Centre for Science and Environment (CSE) assessed the environmental performance of the country's cement industry, covering forty-one companies – 80 per cent of the total. Unexpectedly, it found that air pollution was lower and the industry more energy efficient than in Europe – indeed, second best in the world after Japan. But the sting was in the tail: mining standards were unacceptably poor, with the extraction of limestone 'leading to huge environmental problems, including the depletion of groundwater for local communities'. No fewer than 44 per cent of mines had been set up in ecologically sensitive areas. One of the worst offenders identified by CSE was Associated Cement Companies (ACC), jointly owned by Holcim and India's Ambuja Group, which scored less than 35 per cent on a scale of good performance.[52]

The following year, as the UK government launched yet another waste disposal plan backing co-incineration, the British Society for Ecological Medicine (BSEM) published a report claiming the practice was contrary to international law, which granted citizens the right to a healthy environment. The BSEM alleged that local planners were declaring incinerators safe 'on the basis of out-of-date information and computerised predictions which are no better than tossing a coin'. It confirmed existing research 'strongly suggesting that invisible and unstoppable micro-particles of metals, radioactive materials and medicines are dangerous by-products of incinerators. They get deep into people's lungs and set up reactions which cause birth defects, heart disease and possibly even psychiatric illness, as well as respiratory problems.'[53]

In 2006, Vermont became the first state in the USA (and possibly anywhere) to condemn the burning of tyres for cement production.[54] A little later, just over the border, a powerful coalition of Canadian environmental groups attacked Lafarge and the province of Ontario for their plan to incinerate 'massive amounts of tyres, trash and animal rendering waste in an antiquated cement kiln in Bath, Ontario'. The groups highlighted 'startling increases' in toxic outputs from Lafarge's tyre-burning kiln near Montreal: emissions of cadmium had gone up by 3,064 per cent, of copper by 3,441 per cent, nickel by 1,028 per cent, sulphur dioxide by 145 per cent and particulate matter by 122 per cent.[55]

Can we green houses?

As their promise to deliver 'sustainable cement' fails to convince an increasing number of scientists and communities, so some mining companies are moving towards the promotion of so-called 'sustainable building'. In 2006, UNEP launched a worldwide initiative 'aimed at plugging the gaps in the sustainable building edifice'. Lafarge and Arcelor (now merged with the world's biggest steel producer, L. N. Mittal) are among a dozen companies to have joined the project, pledging to establish 'globally recognised baselines' for 'green building' in order to 'resolve the multiple standards problem'[56] (doubtless a euphemism for lack of enforcement). UNEP says it is 'looking for a common denominator among existing standards, not the more difficult aim of a universal accreditation scheme'. Stephan Schmidheiny's brainchild, the World Business Council for Sustainable Development, has also set up its own three-year project with similar objectives; and Britain's Department for Trade and Industry recently announced 'ten themes for action in the UK', which include the 're-use of existing built assets, designing for minimum waste' and (it goes without saying) 'respect [for] people and their environment'.[57]

It would be premature to dismiss this proliferation of positive-sounding initiatives as a mere smokescreen to cover up the industry's shortcomings. Construction as a whole is held responsible for an estimated 40 per cent of current global wastes. Thus, increased take-up of discarded building materials and the slimming-down of habitable structures should be encouraged. But, since these new codes of practice are voluntary, they so far represent little more than wishful thinking. They are profoundly limited in scope, lacking commitment to examine the life-cycle environmental consequences of using massive amounts of raw materials and of substituting between them (for example, replacing concrete or aluminium with steel, timber with recycled tyres). They also replicate the specious claim, made by cement producers for their own sector, that dangerous wastes from one process can be instantly neutralized simply by inserting them into another. This is a dangerous illusion, increasingly characteristic of other polluters too, as they cast red mud, contaminated with caustic soda from alumina refineries, or fly ash dumped outside power plants, and shot through with heavy metals and radionucleides, into bricks and road surfacing. Above all, the initiatives exclude assessment of the swingeing social costs attached to digging up these materials in the first place. Unless these impacts are urgently addressed, talk of sustainable construction remains at best hot air and, at worst, a monumental confidence trick.

Box 5.2 Fighting back

July 2000: California-based environmental group Friends of the Garcia River successfully quashes a gravel-mining proposal after demonstrating that 'in-stream gravel extraction ruins water quality and destroys habitat for fish, reptiles and birds'.[58]

April 2003–2005: Three Punjabi youths from India, tricked by human traffickers into believing they would get lucrative jobs in Western countries, are instead sold by agents to Lebanese brick kilns in 2003. After further payment for a flight to Istan-

---

bul, they are arrested by the Turkish authorities and sent to Iran, where they suffer three months in jail. Finally they are deported to Pakistan, allowed to spend a year as refugees in a Hindu temple, and returned to India in early 2005.[59]

August 2004: A US federal judge revokes a permit for a Florida limestone mine, agreeing that it would have an adverse impact on a habitat used by the critically endangered Florida panther, only seventy-eight of which still exist within a 2.2-million-acre range. Environmentalists hail the ruling as an important victory 'for a species in serious peril'.[60]

January 2004: Plans to develop Britain's biggest-ever quarry are rejected by the unanimous decision of judges at Edinburgh's Court of Session, after Lafarge fails to overturn a previous executive decision blocking the 600-hectare pit located within a National Scenic Area on the Scottish island of Harris.[61]

2006: 'Courage Village' is established in Pakistan's Punjab province as a safe haven for freed brick kiln and agricultural labourers, thanks to the efforts of peace activist Aslam Khwaja and businessman Kaleem Sheikh.[62]

January 2006: Forty-four bonded labourers, including twenty-eight children, from a brick kiln in Ranchi, capital of the Indian state of Jharkhand, are rescued by police. They were receiving nothing but food for their toil. Police took action after one bonded labourer managed to escape and inform police about the plight of the others.[63]

August 2006: An organization called 'Stop the Quarry Coalition', based in Nova Scotia, Canada, condemns a proposal by US company Bilcon to mine 2 million tonnes of basalt for road surfacing, claiming it will damage the environment, local fishery and tourism. An opposition Liberal member of parliament declares: 'If the door is opened for this to become a gravel pit for the United States, it will be the beginning of the end to a world-class tourist destination.'[64]

Notes

1 P. Madhavan (Mine Labour Protection Campaign) and S. Raj, *Budhpura 'Ground Zero': Sandstone quarrying in India*, Study commissioned by the India Committee of the Netherlands, Amsterdam, 2005, pp. 6–7.

2 *Hindu Business Line*, 25 March 2005.

3 *Financial Times*, 9 September 2005.

4 *Business India*, 12 March 2005.

5 J. Woudhuysen and I. Abbey, *Why is Construction So Backward?*, John Wiley and Sons, Hoboken, NJ, 2004.

6 *Stone Report*, Germany, 21 September 2006.

7 *China Labour Bulletin*, Hong Kong, 30 June 2006.

8 *China Labour Bulletin*, Hong Kong, 18 July 2006.

9 O. Balch, 'Sustainable construction: building momentum, brick by brick', Ethical Corporation (UK), 20 June 2006.

10 Madhavan and Raj, *Budhpura*, p. 12.

11 ILO Conventions governing health and safety in the construction sector include the Safety and Health in Construction Convention of 1988, and the Safety and Health in Mines Convention of 1995, updated in 2006.

12 M. Myuni, 'Dying for a living', *Times of Zambia*, 3 July 2005.

13 This iconic song has sold millions of copies, in various versions, worldwide. Its chorus runs:

'You load sixteen tons, and what do you get?
Another day older and deeper in debt.
Saint Peter, don't you call me, 'cause I can't go;
I owe my soul to the company store.'

14 Madhavan and Raj, *Budhpura*, p. 9.

15 Ibid.

16 Ibid., p. 11.

17 Ibid., p. 16.

18 Ibid., p. 12.

19 Ibid., p. 25.

20 Ibid., p. 23.

21 Ibid., p. 16.

22 Ibid., p. 22.

23 Ibid., p. 24.

24 Ibid., p. 27.

25 *Our Mining Children: A report of the fact finding team on the child labourers in the iron ore and granite mines in Bellary district of Karnataka*, mines, minerals and People (mmP), Hyderabad, April 2005, p. 2.

26 Ibid., p. 4.

27 Ibid., p. 2.

28 Quoted in *Frontline*, Mumbai, March 2005.

29 A. Zaidi, 'Silent victims of silicosis', *Frontline*, Mumbai, 4 November 2005.

30 'Human Rights Commission member visits mining site', NDTV. com, 20 January 2005.

31 *Report of the Justice and Peace Commission (JPC) of Major Superiors Leadership Conference of Pakistan of a Seminar on February 4 2001*, Multan, Pakistan.

32 Ibid.

33 S. Suteville, 'Walking out of slavery', *Indypendent* (New York), 29 June 2006

34 'Human Rights Commission member visits mining site'.

35 L. Smy, 'Hanson faces California sand storm', *Financial Times*, 28 October 2006; see also R. Stevenson, 'Hanson to fight $200m "sand pirate" allegations', *Independent*, London, 28 October 2003.

36 H. Anwar, 'Riau sand exports taking a toll on environment, activists say', *Jakarta Post*, 3 July 2001.

37 S. Kumar, 'Quarrying made Kanyakumari coast vulnerable', *Hindu*, 7 January 2005.

38 *Post-tsunami Assessment Delivers Road Map for Sri Lanka's Sustainable Reconstruction*, Press release by United Nations Environment Programme (UNEP), Colombo, 17 June 2005.

39 G. K. Nair, 'Deforestation, sand mining bring water table down', *Hindu Businessline*, Kochi (Kerala), 5 September 2005.

40 S. Chaturvedi, 'Chrysotile in India: truth held hostage', Editorial, *Indian Journal of Community Medicine*, 31(1).

41 *Financial Times*, 3 August 2006.

42 M. Milstein, 'A faulty formula: the eastern Oregon kiln used for tests leads the DEQ to talk of possible limits on the output', *Oregonian*, 4 August 2006.

43 According to Justin Hayes of the Idaho Conservation Group, data submitted to Nevada regulators by Newmont Mining Co. showed the

The destruction of construction

company's Gold Quarry mine releasing 200 pounds of mercury in 2004, an amount which had grown more than threefold by 2005. At its Twin Creek mine, Newmont reported 300 pounds of mercury releases in 2004 but 600 pounds in 2005. Quoted in J. Fahys, 'Group says mines need to clean act on mercury', *Salt Lake Tribune*, 22 August 2006.

44 Milstein, 'A faulty formula'.

45 See *Schmidheiny and the WBCSD*, Nostromo Research, London, 9 December 2005.

46 'The cement industry and hazardous waste', *Dirt*, Centre for Environmental Protection, London, 2003.

47 P. Brown, 'Rubber solutions', *Guardian*, 4 June 2003, p. 9.

48 A. J. P. Dalton, *Criticism of UK Environment Agency over Alternative Fuels for Cement Kilns: Comments on Review of Agency's Position and Policies on the Use of Substitute Fuels in Cement and Lime Kilns*, Centre for Environmental Protection, Working Lives Research Institute, London Metropolitan University, 2003.

49 Ibid.

50 *German Company Signs First Carbon Finance Deal in Indonesia*, News release, World Bank, Washington, DC.

51 'Call for support', Press inducement to meet demands of fisherfolk of Rampa Jakarta, WALHI (Friends of the Earth, Indonesia), June 2004.

52 *No Concrete Performance*, Press release, Cement Rating Project, Centre for Science and Environment, 31 December 2005.

53 'Doctors urge halt to waste incineration: fallout "harming people and wildlife"', *Yorkshire Post*, 14 February 2006.

54 'Stop burning wastes!', Mines and Communities website, 14 February 2006.

55 *Trashing Lafarge*, Media release, Sierra Legal Defence Fund and Toronto Environmental Alliance, Toronto, 18 May 2006.

56 Balch, 'Sustainable construction'.

57 <www.dti.gov.uk/sectors/construction/sustainability/strategy/page13543.htm>.

58 *AGGREGATES*, July/August 2000, XI(4).

59 *Times of India*, 16 April 2005.

60 J. R. Pegg, Environmental News Service, Washington, DC, 23 August 2004.

61 Scottish Environment LINK Press Release (FoE Scotland), <www.foe-scotland.org.uk/press/pr20040102.html>.

62 Stuteville, 'Walking out of slavery'.

63 'Bonded labourers rescued from brick kiln', *Times of India*, 10 January 2006.

64 J. Keller, *Canadian Press*, 4 August 2006.

6 | Sacrifice areas

The Four Corners region[1] of the US Midwest had, between the late 1940s and early 1980s, been the undisputed epicentre of the global uranium boom. In 1973, the country's Academy of Sciences officially declared the region 'a National Sacrifice area', owing to relentless corporate stripping of its coal, oil, gas and uranium reserves.[2] The term has since been applied around the world; not only to describe the worst that extractive industries can do to land-based peoples, but also in justifying exploitation of their labour.[3] Six years after this trashing of their ancestral territory was officially recognized, Navajos (Dine) living around the Church Rock and Crownpoint mines suffered the worst uranium disaster in US history. A tailings dam burst open in July 1979, sending 1,100 tonnes of mill wastes, and nearly 100 million gallons of radioactive liquids, into Navajo streams and 70 miles down the Rio Puerco, Little Colorado and Colorado rivers.[4] Two dozen years later and the clean-up of those waters is still only 'in progress'.

In 2003, Ben Daitz, professor of medicine at the University of New Mexico School of Medicine, assessed the consequences of the previous sixty years of plunder. '[T]oday more than a thousand abandoned mineshafts still litter this zone,' reported Daitz, 'and five hundred miners, the majority Navajo, are known to have died of lung cancer between 1950 and 1990 when the Radiation Exposure Compensation Act finally introduced compensation for those victimised by mining and nuclear weapons testing.'[5] Native American spokeswoman Winona La Duke reported two years later that 'at least one member of every Navajo family has likely died from lung cancer and other diseases resulting from uranium mining'.[6] Many of the Navajo/Dine miners had to sweat in 'dog holes', crawling along narrow shafts where they constantly inhaled radon 'daughters' as they broke the ore by hand. Others worked in pits owned by 'world class' companies such as Atlantic Richfield (now merged with BP) and Phelps Dodge – today the biggest US copper producer. At these mines safety standards were only marginally better: the Dine still suffered from substandard ventilation, were not afforded face masks and failed to benefit from health and safety checks.

Although the Four Corners region is no longer being plundered to such an extent (having been superceded by bigger uranium mines in Canada and Australia) most Dine have not quit the area: there's nowhere else many of them can afford to go and it is, after all, their tribal land. According to a thesis by John Fogarty, a medical officer with the Indian Health Service, the Dine are acutely vulnerable to the toxic effects of uranium because they have three times the average national propensity to contract diabetes and kidney disease. Despite the energy-seeking companies' assurance that they would leave the underground aquifers safe for drinking, this has not happened.[7] Today residents confront new risks from *in situ* leaching (ISL), bolstered by a US$30 million government subsidy. This technique involves injecting a mixture of water, dissolved oxygen and sodium bicarbonate deep underground, then pumping the liquid back to the surface: a process 'shown to increase the concentrations of uranium and other radioactive elements and heavy metals in the groundwater by up to 100,000 times'.[8] Meanwhile, Peabody Coal, the world's biggest strip miner, has also been accused of depleting water reserves by 50 per cent on both Dine and Hopi land, through its practice of slurrying the coal through pipelines at the rate of 120,000 gallons an hour.[9]

What has happened to the Dine and their neighbours typifies mining practices all over the globe: huge open pits subject to the extremes of drought and flooding (the first causing noxious dusts to blow for miles; the second risking the collapse of waste containment facilities); an absence of basic medical and social facilities; and, in the final event, a total operational failure resulting in degraded agricultural land and toxification or siltation of waterways and streams. At work here is an awesomely simple set of equations: the bigger the mine, then customarily the greater the output of ore. The lower the grade of mineral contained in that ore (and, in general, grades have been diminishing inexorably over the past hundred years) then the higher the levels of surplus rock (overburden), wastes (tailings) discarded from the mill and chemicals used in processing. Unless the wastes are reworked to extract residual economic reserves, they have to be dealt with. At the very least, they should be neutralized of all toxic materials – especially sulphides, which cause 'acid drainage' when exposed to air and water, thus mobilizing heavy metals – then revegetated and contoured. To meet current 'best available' practice criteria they should be detoxified, dried out, compacted, then placed back in the mine, with all leakage points sealed permanently.

Yet, in virtually every locality where mining and minerals processing have recently comprised a major part of the socio-economic fabric, tangible and enduring damage is being done. There are palpable and multiple risks from numerous current mining operations which will inevitably become tomorrow's disaster zones.

Lethal legacies

Today, half a million closed-down mines and mineral operations in the USA are officially recognized as threatening the health and welfare of those living around them. Under a pioneering law passed in 1980, called CERCLA (the Comprehensive Environmental Response, Compensation and Liability Act), the Carter administration set up a National Priorities Superfund List. The Superfund required the Environment Protection Agency (EPA) to ensure 'clean up' of toxic waste sites after polluters went bankrupt, fled or refused to take on the task themselves. Although most of the abandoned sites are industrial ones, the greatest challenges derive from contamination caused by natural resource extraction companies. The mining, manufacturing and industrial sectors are responsible for around 43 per cent of all Superfund sites, while the five most dangerous substances found at these sites (in 2001) are arsenic, lead, mercury, vinyl chloride and polychlorinated biphenyls. A quarter of the population of the United States lives within 4 miles (6.4 kilometres) of a Superfund location, and 85 per cent of them suffer from undrinkable groundwater.

The Superfund has been widely criticized, not least for putting dollars into lawyers' pockets with little visible result and failing to catch polluters before they file for bankruptcy or else abscond. In 2003, the fund was on the verge of exhaustion. Although it formerly provided US$3.8 billion and cleaned up eighty-seven sites a year, in 2003 the Bush administration added only eleven new sites to the National Priorities List, five of which had been used for mining or smelting. This drastic decline was largely due to a decision, made in 1995 by a Republican-controlled Congress, allowing expiry of the 'Polluter Pays' taxes behind the enterprise; the burden of payment then shifted to the general public, which today has to cough up 79 per cent of the costs of the dwindling programme.[10]

In another attempt to hobble the Superfund, the National Mining Association (NMA) in September 2006 sponsored a Congressional draft act which, if passed, would allow miners to organize their own 'remediation' of abandoned sites, while at the same time bypassing existing safeguards imposed by the nation's Clean Water Act, Solid Waste Disposal Act and the Toxic Solutions Control Act. Dubbed by the NMA the 'Good Samaritan' bill, it was clearly designed to allow companies to pass their derelictions by on the other side of the road.[11]

Despite its existing limitations (and the prospect of more), there is no exact parallel to the Superfund anywhere else in the world. Canada has a policy to rehabilitate abandoned (or 'orphaned') mines, of which there are some ten thousand in the country as a whole. Despite this, in December 2005 Ontario's Mines Ministry was slammed by the province's auditor-general for its failure to protect people and environment from the long-term impacts of around half these sites. According to the public watchdog MiningWatch Canada, the auditor general confirmed that

> the mining industry [is allowed] to police itself, while it leaves the public to clean up its mess ... At least 250 of the sites are toxic waste dumps, leaching acidic, metals-contaminated drainage into water courses and aquifers. Many have open adits and shafts, or are contaminated with asbestos. The Auditor-General's findings show that, not only is Ontario doing little to clean up these sites, it is doing almost nothing to prevent more being created.[12]

Among the auditor general's conclusions were that the Mines Ministry 'has no idea of the extent of chemical contamination at more than 4,000 abandoned mine sites, nor does it know what the costs of clean-up will be'. It also 'has no long-term strategy for managing, monitoring and rehabilitating abandoned mines. Of the 144 mines for which a plan to remediate the mine after closure should be in place, 18 have no plan at all.' Although required to provide financial insurance (a bond) to make sufficient clean-up funds available if they don't or can't do it themselves, the ministry 'relies on mining companies themselves to assess and certify the amount of security they must provide'. In many cases, firms with a Triple B, or higher, credit rating are allowed to 'self-assure' – in other words to post no bond at all. In nineteen cases, companies have been allowed to contribute to a 'sinking

Sacrifice areas

fund' instead of posting the bond. Four others were allowed to go bankrupt without having paid even a minimum $600,000 into the fund. Almost half the sites – nearly two thousand of them – had not even been inspected in the previous five years.[13]

Elsewhere around the world, communities residing close to hundreds of thousands of other derelict mines are still waiting to benefit from the minimal requirements of US and Canadian regulations; the European Union did not introduce its 'Seveso II' standards for clean-up until 2005. The global total of inactive sites has never been methodically assessed, although we know that the small country of Namibia (population just over 2 million) is officially burdened with 240 abandoned mines[14] and, on the small South Pacific island of Nauru, four-fifths of the surface area remains unreclaimed, following a century of relentless phosphates excavation principally by Australia, New Zealand and the UK. At the end of 2005, while Philippine NGOs alleged that 857 abandoned mines were causing health and environmental problems, it is anyone's guess as to the true dimensions of similar toxic chemical and metal burdens, accompanied by soil and water degradation, to be found across the rest of Asia, Russia, Africa and Latin America.[15]

Two recent surveys do, however, give a clue. Neither of them was focused specifically on natural resource extraction, but are all the more significant for that. They not only expose mining and minerals processing as highly detrimental to our global well-being; in several regions these are demonstrated to be the biggest culprits. A 2003 'Loss and Litigation' report published by the world's fourth-largest reinsurer, General ReCologne, named major corporate environmental offenders in twenty countries. It also warned of an alarming rise in incidences of chemical pollution, as logged by the European Union's MARS (Major Accident Reporting System). Such cases almost quadrupled between 1985 and 1998 (up from a dozen to fifty-seven), despite a plethora of avowedly stringent preventative legislation introduced over those thirteen years. Equally disturbing was the proportion of mining-related cases on General Re's list – at fourteen, these comprised a quarter of the total.[16]

Six years later, in October 2006, the well-reputed US-based Blacksmith Institute went one step farther. Out of thirty-five front-line candidates it dared to pick the 'world's ten worst polluted places', based on research by a team with 'over 250 years of combined experience in this field [including] specialists from Johns Hopkins, Hunter College, Harvard University, IIT India, University of Idaho, Mt Sinai Hospital, and leaders of major international environmental remediation companies'.[17] Blacksmith's board made its selection based upon the size of the affected population; severity of the toxin or toxins involved; impact on children's health and development; evidence of a clear pathway of contamination; and 'existing and reliable evidence of health impact'. It freely admitted a bias 'towards including point source and legacy issues' and a 'desire to include representative sites for certain types of pollution, and sites that document the global span of such problems'. While refraining from 'pointing a finger at one place ... saying that this is the worst on earth', and while agreeing that its nominees were 'by no means isolated or unique', Blacksmith reasonably proposed that 'being on the final list of ten is bad enough'.[18]

What stands out head and shoulders above all the other evidence presented by the institute is the huge amount of damage (especially to young people) wreaked by mining, metallic processing and the burning of coal. In fact, these specific point sources were responsible for no fewer than 80 per cent of the ten 'world's worst' contaminated and contaminating sites. Five of them have already been closed: the Haina lead smelter in the Dominican Republic; the Kabwe lead operations in Zambia; a sprawl of uranium mines and mills in Kyrgyzstan; the Rudnaya

Pristan lead works in Russia; and a tanneries complex at Ranipet, India, which dumped chromium and chromate wastes – 1.5 million (*sic*) tonnes of it – in just one corner of Tamil Nadu. Shut down they may be, but the toxic legacy of these operations is extremely severe, with some of them defying the capacities of any current clean-up technology. In one case (Kabwe) discharges from a copper tailings leach plant, operated by UK-listed Vedanta Resources, were identified in 2006 as still contributing to poisoning of the region's main river.[19]

Blacksmith's other three chosen top felons continue very much to offend: the Norilsk complex in Russia; Doe Run's La Oroya smelter in Peru; and the authorities in China's Shanxi province as they permit a complex of coal mines, coal-fired power utilities, steel and tar plants.

A cursory perusal of the Blacksmith data might suggest that lead mining, refining and usage is currently the worst single threat to life and health on this planet. That would be a major error, failing to take into account the impacts of a wide range of other radioactive and heavy metals, some of which may be deadlier in the short run (such as mercury and arsenic), or claim a far wider range of victims in the longer term (for example, asbestos). The institute estimates that 3.5 million people at Ranipet in India are – or will be – damaged by leakages of hexavalent chromium and related wastes at the present rate of removal (or rather, lack of it).

Data on the impacts of the minerals sector, compiled by Blacksmith from a fuller shortlist of thirty-five cases, ranked India worst overall (with over 3 million people suffering or at risk), followed by Russia (nearly 3 million). The Philippines (200,000) and Zambia (250,000) match China (200,000), while the potential number of sufferers from a failure to clean up Kyrgyzstan's uranium tailings could, says Blacksmith, range from 23,000 to 'millions'. Moreover, an estimated 150,000 citizens of Romania

are reckoned to be suffering from the impacts of just two operations: the Baie Marie tailings disaster of 2000 and emissions from
an old base metals smelter; while nearly 1 per cent of citizens in
the Dominican Republic (population around 9 million) are also
said to be suffering various degrees of poisoning from another
lead smelter.

The world's worst places 2006

Blacksmith identified the following eight mining and mineral-
related cases among the 'world's worst ten'. (The text below is
drawn from the institute's own summary.)

China: coal mining/steel smelting: Linfen, Shanxi Province

Potential population affected: 200,000

Type of pollutants: Fly-ash, carbon monoxide, nitrogen oxides,
PM-2.5, PM-10, sulfur dioxide, volatile organic compounds, arsenic,
lead

High levels of pollution are taking a serious toll on the health
of Linfen's inhabitants. Local clinics are seeing growing cases of
bronchitis, pneumonia, and lung cancer. Lead poisoning was also
observed at very high rates in Chinese children in Shanxi Province.
Levels of SO_2 and other particulates in the air exceed many times
over the standards set by the World Health Organization. A growing
number of resident deaths in recent years have been directly linked
to this intense pollution. Compounding the problem is the city's
economic dependence on the coal, steel, and tar industries, as
well as China's need for these resources in keeping with its rapidly
growing economy. As with many environmental problems in China,
strong resistance from business interests and corrupt officials has
made improvement difficult to imagine in a short timeframe: Information on progress towards cleanup in this area is not currently
readily available.

Sacrifice areas

Kabwe, Zambia: lead mining

Potentially affected people: 250,000

Type of pollutants: Lead, cadmium

Kabwe, the second largest city in Zambia, is located about 150 kilometers north of the nation's capital, Lusaka. On average, children's blood levels in Kabwe are 5 to 10 times the allowable EPA maximum. Mining and smelting operations were running almost continuously up until 1994 without the government addressing the potential danger of lead. The smelting process was unregulated during this period and the smelters released heavy metals in dust particles, which settled on the ground in the surrounding area. The mine and smelter is no longer operating but has left a city poisoned from debilitating concentrations of lead in the soil and water from slag heaps that were left as reminders to the smelting and mining era. In one study, the dispersal in soils of lead, cadmium, copper, and zinc extended to over a 20 km circumference from the smelting and mining processes. In some neighborhoods, blood concentrations of 200 or more micrograms/deciliter have been recorded in children, while records show average blood levels of children range between 50 and 100 mcg/dl. Children who play in the soil and young men who scavenge the mines for scraps of metal are most susceptible to lead produced by the mine and smelter.

After decades of contamination, the cleanup strategy for Kabwe is complex and in its primary stages. The first step is to educate the community about the risks of lead poisoning and their susceptibility to the pollutant. Some areas of Kabwe require drastic remediation in which some entire neighborhoods may need to relocate. The World Bank has approved a $20 million grant to clean up the city and has just completed the scoping study that will lead to initial cleanup activity beginning in 2007.

Norilsk, Russia: nickel, cobalt, cadmium, platinum group metals; mining refining and smelting

Potentially affected people: 134,000

Type of pollutants: Air pollution – particulates including strontium-90, caesium-137, sulfur dioxide, heavy metals (nickel, copper, cobalt, lead, selenium), particulates, nitrogen and carbon oxides, phenols, hydrogen sulfide

An industrial city founded in 1935 as a slave labor camp, the Siberian city of Norilsk, Russia is the northernmost major city of Russia and the second largest city (after Murmansk) above the Arctic Circle. According to the Mines and Communities website the city is considered one of the most polluted places in Russia – where the snow is black, the air tastes of sulfur and the life expectancy for factory workers is 10 years below the Russian average. This city houses the world's largest heavy metals smelting complex, and over 4 million tons annually of cadmium, copper, lead, nickel, arsenic, selenium and zinc are dispersed into the air. Mining and smelting operation started in the 1930s and Norilsk is the world's largest nickel producer – a recently privatized firm which ranks first among Russian industrial enterprises in terms of air pollution. Due to the geographic location, reports on ecological impacts and contamination are infrequent from this location. In 1999, a report found elevated copper and nickel concentrations in soils up to a 60 km radius; investigations evaluating the presence of ear, nose and throat disease among schoolchildren revealed that children living near the copper plant were twice as likely to become ill as those living in further districts.

Since November 2001, Norilsk has been shut to foreigners, one of 90 'closed towns' in Russia where Soviet-levels of secrecy persist. Many groups, some supported by international donors, have tried to address the problems. In the 1980's, emission reductions were tried by building dust and gas removal facilities, but studies prove that damage to forests and concentrations of metals remained a significant problem to date.

Sacrifice areas

137

Haina, Dominican Republic: lead smelter ('recycling')

Potentially affected people: 85,000

Type of pollutants: Lead, lead emissions from smelter

This highly populated area known as Bajos de Haina is severely contaminated with lead from a closed-down automobile battery recycling smelter. The Dominican Secretary of Environment and Natural Resources, since its creation in 2000, has identified Haina as a national hotspot of significant concern. Various studies have found alarming lead levels in the Haina community, with blood and soil levels several orders of magnitude over regular limits. Although the Metaloxa battery plant has moved to a new site (which is contaminating another neighborhood, albeit less populous), the contamination still remains. Birth deformities, eye damage, learning and personality disorders, and in some cases, death from lead poisoning, have also been reported at a higher than normal rate due to contamination caused by the past operations of the battery plant. Cleanup activity is in early planning stages, with Blacksmith Institute advice and support.

La Oroya, Peru: polymetallic smelter

Potentially affected people: 35,000

Type of pollutants: Lead, copper, zinc, and sulfur dioxide

Since 1922, adults and children in La Oroya, Peru – a mining town in the Peruvian Andes and the site of a polymetallic smelter – have been exposed to the toxic emissions from the plant. Currently owned by the Missouri-based Doe Run Corporation, the plant is largely responsible for the dangerously high blood lead levels found in the children of this community. Ninety-nine percent of children living in and around La Oroya have blood lead levels that exceed acceptable levels, according to studies carried out by the Director General of Environmental Health in Peru in 1999. Sulfur dioxide concentrations also exceed the World Health Organization emissions standards ten fold. The vegetation in the surrounding area has been destroyed by acid rain, due to high SO_2 emissions. To date, the extent of soil contamination has not been studied and no plan for reduction of emissions has been agreed or implemented. Numerous studies have been carried out to assess the levels and sources of lead and other metals still being deposited in La Oroya. Limited testing has revealed lead, arsenic and cadmium soil contamination throughout the town. However, all of these studies were focused on outdoor contamination and suspected severe indoor air pollution has not yet been assessed in detail. Peru's Clean Air Act cites La Oroya in a list of Peruvian towns suffering critical levels of air pollution, but action to clean up and curtail this pollution has been delayed for the 35,000 inhabitants. In 2004, Doe Run Corporation asked the government for a four-year extension to the plant's environmental management plan. A concerted NGO movement is now underway to pressure the company and the government to develop effective strategies for implementation of site remediation agreements and to provide health care for affected residents.

Ranipet, India: chromium manufacture

Potentially affected people: 3,500,000

Type of pollutants: Tannery waste, containing hexavalent chromium and azodyes

Ranipet is located about 100 miles upstream from Chennai, the fourth largest urban area in India. Although Ranipet is a medium sized town, its problems also pose a potential risk to the population of the nearby city of Vellore. A factory in Ranipet manufactures sodium chromate, chromium salts and basic chromium sulfate tanning powder used locally in the leather tanning process. The Tamil Nadu Pollution Control Board (TNPCB) estimates that about 1,500,000 tons of solid wastes, accumulated over two decades of plant operation, are stacked in an open yard (three to five meters high, occupying 2 hectares of land) on the facility premises, and contaminating the groundwater. The contamination of the soil and

Sacrifice areas

139

groundwater with wastewater, as well as run off from solid wastes, has affected the health, resources, and livelihood of thousands of people. In a residential colony about 1 kilometer from the factory three open wells, a dozen bore wells and 25 public hand pumps have been abandoned due to high chromium levels in the water. In 1996 the government shut down Tamil Nadu Chromates & Chemicals Limited (TCC), the factory responsible for an estimated 1.5 million tons of untreated chromate sludge. The TNPCB has assigned the National Geophysical Research Institute (NGRI) and National Environmental Engineering Research Institute (NEERI) to design and implement remediation plans to clean up this site. An effective solution to tackle the issue of chromate leaching from the legacy site would be to encapsulate the waste dumpsite to prevent further leaching and treating the subsurface soil of the channel-flows.

Rudnaya Pristan/Dalnegorsk, Russia: lead smelter

Potentially affected people: 90,000

Type of pollutants: Lead, cadmium, mercury, antimony

Dalnegorsk and Rudnaya Pristan are two towns in the Russian Far East whose residents suffer serious lead poisoning from an old smelter and the unsafe transport of lead concentrate from the local lead mining site. According to the most recent study, lead concentrations in residential gardens (476–4310 mg/kg, Gmean=1626 mg/kg) and in roadside soils (2020–22900 mg/kg, Gmean=4420 mg/kg) exceed USEPA guidance for remediation by orders of magnitude. These data suggest that drinking water, interior dust, and garden crops also likely contain dangerous levels of lead. Water discharged from the smelter averages 2900 m³/day with concentrations up to 100 kg of lead and 20 kg arsenic.

Limited initial testing has revealed that children's blood lead levels are 8 to 20 times the maximum allowable U.S. levels. Preliminary bio kinetic estimates of mean blood levels suggest that preschool children are at significant risk of lead poisoning from soil/dust ingestion with levels predicted to average 13–27 microg/dl. Annual air emissions found 5 tons of particulate matter with lead and arsenic concentrations being 50 and 0.5 tons, respectively. Since 1930 there has not been any attempt to address associated health concerns by either an educational or a technical environmental program. In fact, the residents of the area were simply left to deal with health risk problems on their own and are largely unaware of the risks. Furthermore, some residents in Rudnaya use old casings of submarine batteries that were recycled by the smelter in order to collect precipitation for watering their gardens.

The lead smelter has now been voluntarily shut down, after Blacksmith presented the owner with data on the health risks to children of lead contamination. In addition, children's blood lead levels are being tested, and those with elevated levels are being treated with Blacksmith funding. This funding has also supported a program of education to all residents, and local education and testing through the community is ongoing. Next, a plan to remediate the worst of the contamination needs to be drawn up and implemented.

Mailuu-Suu, Kyrgyzstan: uranium mining

Potentially affected people: 23,000 immediate, millions potentially

Type of pollutants: Radioactive uranium mine tailings. Gamma radiation from the dumps measures in between 100–600 microroentgens per hour. Heavy metals, and cyanides

There are twenty-three tailing dumps and thirteen waste rock dumps scattered throughout Mailuu-Suu, home to a former Soviet uranium plant. From 1946–1968 the plant produced and processed more than 10,000 metric tons of uranium ore, products which were eventually used to produce the Soviet Union's first atomic bomb. What remains now are not atomic bombs, but 1.96 million cubic meters of radioactive mining waste that threatens the entire

Ferghana valley, one of the most fertile and densely populated area in Central Asia.

Due to the high rates of seismic activity in the area, millions of people in Central Asia are potentially at risk from a failure of the waste containment. Natural hazards, such as earthquakes, landslides, and mudflows, all have the potential to exacerbate problems associated with the location and mismanagement of these tailing piles. It is feared that a landslide could disturb one of the dumps and either expose radioactive material within the core of the enormous waste piles or push part of them into nearby rivers. This fear was nearly realized in May of 2002 when a huge mudslide blocked the course of the Mailuu-Suu river and threatened to submerge another waste site. In April 2006, the *Obschestvenny Reiting* newspaper reported that about 300,000 cubic meters of material fell into the Mailuu-Suu river near the uranium mine tailings, the result of yet another landslide. Events such as these could potentially contaminate water drunk by hundreds of thousands of people in the Ferghana valley, shared by Kyrgyzstan, Uzbekistan and Tajikistan.

The poor design and management of the waste areas also allows transfer of some material from these piles to surrounding areas by runoff. Research has found some groups getting very high doses of radon probably due to use of this runoff water in agriculture. Risk analyses have also been conducted to assess the radioactive contamination that could occur with more natural disasters, and have found these could lead to potential large-scale environmental contamination. A 1999 study conducted by the Institute of Oncology and Radioecology showed that twice as many residents suffered from some form of cancer than in the rest of the country. The World Bank has begun a project for Kyrgyzstan to 'minimize the exposure of humans, livestock, and riverine flora and fauna to radionuclide associated with abandoned uranium mine tailings and waste rock dumps in the Mailuu-Suu area'. The project includes uranium mining wastes' isolation and protection, improvement to the national system for disaster management, preparedness and response and the establishment of real-time monitoring and warning systems, seismic stations and sensors. The total cost of the project is 11.76 million U.S. dollars, of which the bank's International Development Association will provide 6.9 million dollars.

Poisoned chalices

It is clear from the unique Blacksmith study that, while efforts are being made to mitigate the impacts of some past disasters, in fact none of them is incidental and many are systemic, demanding massive applications of both money and political will in order to avoid continuing damage. If two of the best-heeled democracies on earth cannot muster enough funding and application to ameliorate their own past misdemeanours, then what are the prospects for (say) India and China? Industry spokespeople argue that such disasters would be unthinkable today were voluntary principles strictly enforced and government oversight more stringent. In reality, mines continue to be constructed in the midst of farming communities, or bang up against urban settlements – as in Jamaica and India, where bauxite dust blows into homes and schools.[20] Two operational copper-gold mines (Grasberg in West Papua and Ok Tedi in Papua New Guinea) carry on inundating entire river systems with their wastes, threatening degradation from which recovery may not be achieved even decades after mining officially stops. Ejecting tailings on to the ocean floor (where they can, and do, well up into local fishing grounds) is defended by three major companies, Rio Tinto, Barrick/Placer and Newmont Mining; several smaller outfits, including Norway-based Crew Resources in the Philippines, have plans to do the same.

Above all, the direst of events that face a mining operation are happening to this day with appalling regularity and no sign of abating. There are few occurrences more dramatic, or traumatic, than the collapse of a mine tailings dam or slag heap. After a coal dump slid down a mountain on to the Welsh village of Aberfan, on 21 October 1966, culling an entire community (116 of the 144 victims were primary school children), it was universally acknowledged to be Britain's most severe industrial-related socio-environmental disaster. Following the breach of Omai Gold's dam wall in 1995, Guyana's head of state, Cheddi Jagan, declared this too as the nation's 'worst ever environmental disaster'.[21] When an Australian company's Romanian tailings dam overflowed in February 2000, the Hungarian government called it 'the largest environmental disaster in central Europe in thirty years'.[22]

Not surprisingly, it is Chinese citizens who have fared worst of all from such calamities. This doesn't mean, however, that China is uniquely vulnerable. Fourteen South Africans died during just one night in 1994, when heavy rains caused a breach in the gold slimes dam at Merriespruit. The following year, a similar breakout at a Philippine gold mine buried twelve residents alive. The USA has recorded nine significant failures over the past fifteen years, though fortunately none resulted in serious human injury. In 2004, 60 million gallons of acidic water gushed into a Florida creek as Hurricane Frances struck a 100-foot gypsum stack at a phosphate mine; the news hardly ruffled the press. In contrast, the overflow of cyanide-contaminated waters from a Romanian gold recovery facility in early 2000 (mentioned above) sent headlines across the world. Almost immediately, drinking water for 2 million people downstream in Hungary was profoundly contaminated: the European Union's Environment Commissioner determined 'the whole of the Danube [to be] polluted with cyanide'.[23] Just over five weeks later another huge cocktail of heavy metals burst from a similar Romanian facility and into a local stream.

A few agencies try keeping track of such 'incidents'. One of them is the World Information Service on Energy (WISE), originally set up to monitor the nuclear/uranium industry. The following section provides a summary of the most worrisome of these disasters from 1991 to 2006, based on WISE's research and other sources. Some of the data are conjectural and we should not be dazzled by figures alone. A few spillages appear to have been swiftly contained while others pose a clear and very present danger. Nevertheless, what stands out is the large number of countries affected (eighteen in all) and the fact that seven of these are states that should have the technology to prevent, or at least mitigate, such catastrophes. For example, one of the worst took place in Cornwall at a closed mine, previously managed by Rio Tinto and supposedly being checked by the UK Environment Agency. (What better credentials could one hope for?)

Even more striking is the regularity of these occurrences over a decade and a half, and right up until the present. According to the European Commission, 'at world level [tailings dams] have failed at an average of 1.7 per year over the past 30 years'. Of equal concern is the number of major corporations supposedly managing the mines right up until the point at which they became a major social and environmental threat. As well as Rio Tinto, these include BHPBilliton, Teck Cominco (the world's leading zinc producer), Boliden (Sweden's major mining company) WMC of Australia (now part of BHPBilliton), France's nuclear-uranium company, Areva, and Harmony Gold of South Africa.

Fourteen years of failure, 1992–2006[24]

The following chronology does not take into account recent cyanide and other major toxic metals leaks which have fallen short of a partial or complete collapse of the engineered tailings or wastes dam. There were at least twenty-eight such incidents between August 1995 and June 2006: no fewer than eight in Ghana; three in Romania/Hungary and the USA; two in China, Australia, the Philippines and Guyana; and one each in Laos,

Papua New Guinea, Nicaragua, Aotearoa/New Zealand, Honduras and the Czech Republic.[25]

April 30 2006 near Miliang, Zhen'an County, Shangluo, Shaanxi Province, China: Zhen'an County Gold Mining Co. Ltd's tailings dam fails during a sixth upraising of the dam. The resulting landslide buries about forty rooms in nine households, leaving seventeen residents missing. Five injured people are taken to hospital. More than 130 local residents are evacuated. Toxic potassium cyanide is released into the Huashui river, contaminating it for some 5 kilometres downstream.

April 14 2005 at Bangs Lake, Jackson County, Mississippi, USA: Mississippi Phosphates Corp.'s phosphor-gypsum stack founders, because the company was trying to increase the capacity of the pond at a faster rate than normal, according to officials with the Mississippi Department of Environmental Quality, although the company blames the spill on unusually heavy rainfall. Around 17 million gallons of acidic liquid ($64,350m^3$) pours into adjacent marshlands, causing vegetation to die.

November 30 2004 at Pinchi Lake, British Columbia, Canada: Teck Cominco Ltd's mercury tailings impoundment (100 metres long and 12 metres high) collapses during reclamation work, with the result that $6,000–8,000m^3$ of rock, dirt and waste water tailings spill into the 5,500-hectare Pinchi Lake.

September 5 2004 at Riverview, Florida, USA: Cargill Crop Nutrition's phosphate dyke at the top of a 100-foot-high gypsum stack, holding 150 million gallons of polluted water, sunders after waves driven by Hurricane Frances bash the dyke's south-west corner. Sixty million gallons ($227,000m^3$) of acidic liquid spills into Archie Creek, which leads to Hillsborough Bay.

May 22 2004 at Partizansk, Primorski Krai, Russia: Dalenergo's ring dyke, enclosing an area of roughly 1km² and holding about 20 million cubic metres of coal ash, breaks. It leaves a hole roughly 50 metres wide in the dam and approximately 160,000 cubic metres of ash gushes through a drainage canal into a tributary to the Partizanskaya river, which empties into Nahodka Bay in Primorski Krai (east of Vladivostok).

March 20 2004 at Malvési, Aude, France: Comurhex (Cogéma/ Areva)'s decantation and evaporation pond at its uranium conversion plant dam fails after heavy rains the preceding year. The release of 30,000m³ of liquid and slurries leads to elevated nitrate concentrations of up to 170mg/L in the Tauran canal for several weeks following.

October 3 2003 at Cerro Negro, Petorca province, Quinta region, Chile: a rift in Cia Minera Cerro Negro's copper tailings dam sends 50,000 tonnes of tailings 20 kilometres downstream into the Río La Ligua.

August 27–September 11 2002 at San Marcelino, Zambales, Philippines: Dizon Copper Silver Mines, Inc. experiences an overflow and spillway failure at two abandoned tailings dams after heavy rain. Some tailings enter Mapanuepe Lake and eventually the Santo Tomas river. Low-lying villages are inundated with mine waste; 250 families are evacuated; nobody is reported injured.

June 22 2001 at Sebastião das Águas Claras, Nova Lima district, Minas Gerais, Brazil: Mineração Rio Verde Ltda's iron mill tailings dam fails, causing a wave of wastes to travel at least 6 kilometres, killing at least two mineworkers; three others are reported 'missing'.

October 18 2000 in Nandan county, Guangxi province, China: reported tailings dam collapse killing at least fifteen people, with 100 unaccounted for and more than 100 houses destroyed.

October 11 2000 at Inez, Martin County, Kentucky, USA: Martin County Coal Corporation sustains a coal slurry containment failure as an underground mine collapses beneath the impoundment: 250 million gallons (950,000m³) of wastes flow into neighbouring streams. About 75 miles (120 kilometres) of rivers and streams turn an iridescent black, killing fish along the Tug Fork of the Big Sandy river and some of its tributaries. Towns along the Tug are forced to turn off their drinking water intakes.

September 8 2000 at the Aitik mine, Gällivare, Sweden: following a dam failure due to blockage of a filter drain, copper tailings containing 2.5 million m³ of liquid are released into an adjacent settling pond; with the subsequent release of 1.5 million m³ of water (carrying some residual slurry) from the settling pond into the environment.

March 10 2000 at Borsa, Romania: Remin SA's tailings dam fails during heavy rains: 22,000 tonnes of heavy-metal-contaminated wastes enter the Vaser stream, a tributary of the Tisza river.

January 20 2000 at Baia Mare, Romania: the crest of a dam, used by Aurul SA, jointly owned by Esmeralda Exploration of Australia (50 per cent) and Remin SA (44.8 per cent), to recover gold from tailings, collapses owing to rains and melted snow. The overflow, containing 100,000m³ of liquids contaminated with up to 120 tonnes of cyanide and heavy metals, travels downstream into the Rivers Somes and Tisa, then into Hungary before entering the Danube, killing tonnes of fish and poisoning the drinking water of more than 2 million people. According to the Blacksmith Institute's 'World's Worst Places' report of October 2006 (see p. 135), 140,000 people still remain at risk.

April 26 1999 in Surigao del Norte, Philippines: owing to rupture of a concrete pipe at a Manila Mining Corp. mine, 700,000 tonnes of cyanide tailings bury seventeen homes and swamp 51 hectares of rice land.

December 31 1998 in Huelva, Spain: during a storm, the failure of Fertiberia's phosphate dam results in the release of 50,000m^3 of acidic and toxic waters.

April 25 1998 at Los Frailes, Aznalcóllar, Spain: Boliden Ltd's zinc, lead, copper and silver tailings dam is struck by a foundation failure; 4–5 million m^3 of toxic water and slurry covers thousands of hectares of farmland and also enters the Donana National Park. The mine reopened a year later, despite vigorous protests from environmental groups and park management.

December 7 1997 at Phosphate, Polk County, Florida: USA Mulberry Phosphates Inc.'s phospho-gypsum stack collapses, releasing 200,000m^3 of process water which eliminates all biota in the Alafia river.

October 22 1997 in Pinto Valley, Arizona, USA: a slope failure at BHP Copper's dam results in the dispersal of 230,000m^3 of rock and tailings which cover 16 hectares of adjacent land.

November 12 1996 at Amatista, Nazca, Peru: an apparent liquefaction failure in the upstream-type dam during an earthquake propels more than 300,000m^3 of tailings in a run-out of about 600 metres, spilling into a nearby river and contaminating crops.

August 29 1996 along the El Porco river, Bolivia: after a dam breach at a zinc, lead and silver mine operated by Comsur (62 per cent privately owned by then president 'Goni' Lozado and a third by Rio Tinto), around 400,000 tonnes of tailings contaminate up to 300 kilometres of the Pilcomayo river and adjacent agriculture.

March 24 1996 on Marinduque Island, Philippines: following the failure of a 'plug', holding back old tailings in a storage pit, 1.6 million m^3 of copper tailings burst through a disused drainage tunnel, ruining farmland; 1,200 residents are evacuated, 18 kilometres of river channel are clogged with tailings and the neighbouring bay is smothered. At least US$80 million of damage is caused. Criminal charges are brought against the Philippine company Marcopper, of which Canada's Placer Dome owns 40 per cent. In the ten years since, no effective method has been devised to retrieve and safely dispose of the wastes.

September 2 1995 in Surigao del Norte, Philippines: Manila Mining Corp.'s gold tailings dam founders and twelve people are buried alive under 50,000m^3 of wastes, which also blanket part of the coastline.

August 19 1995 at Omai, Guyana: a gold tailings impoundment at the eponymous mine – jointly owned by Cambior Inc. – (65 per cent), Golden Star Resources Inc. (30 per cent) and the Guyana government (5 per cent) – suddenly develops a massive crack, caused by internal erosion; 4.2 million m^3 of cyanide and heavy-metals-bearing slurry are carried 80 kilometres down the Essequibo river and towards the ocean. President Cheddi Jagan calls this 'the country's worst environmental disaster'.

November 19 1994 at the Hopewell Mine, Hillsborough County, Florida: a failure of IMC-Agrico's phosphate containment facility results in almost 1.9 million m^3 of water from a clay settling pond spilling into nearby wetlands and the Alafia river.

October 2 1994 at the Payne Creek Mine, Polk County, Florida, USA: in an uncanny foreshadowing of the 19 November 'incident', IMC-Agrico's phosphate dam collapses, releasing 6.8 million m^3 of water from a clay settling pond. Most of the discharge is contained in an adjacent mining area; however, 500,000m^3 goes into Hickey Branch, a tributary of Payne Creek.

February 22 1994 at the Harmony Gold mine site, Merriespruit, South Africa: a breach in the dam wall, following heavy rains, causes 600,000m³ tailings to plunge 4 kilometres downstream. Seventeen local residents are killed and there is extensive damage to the township. Later criminal charges are successfully brought against the company.

1993 at Marsa, Peru: the Marsa Mining Corp.'s gold dam sustains a failure, probably from 'overtopping', and six people are reported killed.

March 1 1992 at Maritsa Istok 1, near Stara Zagora, Bulgaria: following a reported ash/cinder dam failure, a nearby beach is inundated with around 500,000m³ of wastes.

January 1992 in Cornwall, south-west England: the closed Wheal Jane tin mine dam bursts its banks after underground water overflows from underground shafts. The arsenic-, zinc-, cadmium- and mercury-primed wastes sweep down the River Fal into the coastal estuary, turning the river red and smothering most of the 4,000-acre oyster beds.

January 1992 at Padcal, Luzon, Philippines: Philex Mining Corp.'s number 2 dam wall ruptures, with a spill of 80 million tonnes of copper tailings.

Notes

1 So called because it marks the meeting point of the states of Utah, Colorado, Arizona and New Mexico.

2 L. Proyect, 'Marxism, ecology and the American Indians' (in manuscript), University of Columbia, 1999.

3 In her autobiography the nuclear critic Helen Broinowski Caldicott accuses the Nixon administration of basing its energy policy around the mining of national sacrifice areas. See H. B. Caldicott, *A Desperate Passion; an Autobiography*, Norton, New York, 1996.

4 H. Wasserman, N. Solomon with R. Alvarez and E. Walter, *Killing Our Own: The Disaster of America's Experience with Atomic Radiation*, Delta Books, New York, 1982.

5 B. Daitz, 'Navajo miners battle a deadly legacy of yellow dust', *New York Times*, 5 May 2003.

6 W. La Duke, 'Uranium ban – leading the way into the new millennium', Draft paper, White Earth reservation, 2005. See also W. La Duke, *Indigenous Peoples, Power & Politics*, Honor the Earth Publications, Minneapolis, MN, 2004.

7 Diatz, 'Navajo miners'.

8 La Duke, 'Uranium ban'.

9 National Resources Defense Council, 'Drawdown: an update on groundwater mining on Black Mesa', New York, March 2006.

10 Sources for the Superfund data cited in this book include: 'Superfund drastically depleted', *Oregonian*, 11 August 2003; 'Maryland environmental group attacks under funding of Superfund by Bush Administration', *Daily Record*, 8 August 2003; 'Jeffords critical of Superfund funding decision', *Real Estate/Environmental Liability News*, 1 August 2003; Jim Geraghty, 'EPA won't fund waste cleanups in Mass., N.H. sites', States News Service, 22 July 2003; 'Real communities, real people, real threats' and 'Superfund's Polluter Pays fees', Superfund fact sheets, Campaign to Clean Up Toxics, US Public Interest Research Group; National Priorities List fact sheet, 'Projects receiving fiscal year 2003 new funding', Superfund website, Environmental Protection Agency.

11 'Bad Polluted Mine Bill would shield polluter under guise of "Good Samaritan"', Press release, Earthjustice, Oakland, CA, 13 September 2006.

12 'Ontario Auditor-General slams Mines Ministry over failure to protect the public', Press statement by MiningWatch Canada, Ontario, 7 December 2005.

13 Ibid.

14 *Mining Journal*, London, 26 March 2003.

15 '857 abandoned mines pose health menace, say NGOs', ABS-CBN Interactive, 11 October 2005.

16 R. Moody, *The Risks We Run: Mining, Communities and Political Risk Insurance*, International Books, Utrecht, 2005, p. 50.

17 'World's worst polluted places', Blacksmith Institute, New York, 2006.

18 Ibid.

19 'Zambia: lead poisoning concern in mining town', 2005, <www.minesandcommunities.org/Action/press568.htm>.

20 C. J. Williams, 'Dust up swirls around Jamaican industry', *Los Angeles Times*, 14 October 2004; R. Moody and N. Jayaraman et al., *Ravages through India: Vedanta Resources plc Counter Report*, Nostromo Research, London, with India Resource Center, San Francisco, CA, 2005, pp. 9–12.

21 R. Moody, *Into the Unknown Regions: The Hazards of STD*, Society of St Columban and International Books, London and Utrecht, 2001, p. 48.

22 Ibid.

23 'Proposal for a Directive of the European Parliament and of the Council, amending Council Directive 96/82/EC of December 9 1996 on the control of major accident hazards involving dangerous substances', COM (20010 624), updated on 26 October 2004.

24 This list is compiled from three main sources: the World Information Service on Energy (WISE) Chronology of Major Dam Failures, 9 May 2006; R. Moody, *Into the Unknown Regions* and 'Proposal for a Directive of the European Parliament and of the Council amending Council Directive 96/82/EC'.

25 Data supplied by the Rainforest Information Centre, Lismore, Australia, 2006.

Sacrifice areas

7 | Winning hearts and mines

> 'The twentieth century has been characterised by three develop-
> ments of great political importance: the growth of democracy, the
> growth of corporate power and the growth of corporate propaganda
> as a means of protecting corporate power against democracy.'[1]

John Bray, research head at Control Risks, the world's biggest
advisory agency on corporate risk-taking, used to tell clients that
so long as they secured 'dialogue' with their critics 'then you
win'. However, 'if you meet a group that will not compromise,
then you have a problem'.[2] It's a lesson the minerals industry
has finally learned after bitter experience stretching back more
than forty years. Nevertheless, it was not until 1989 that one
of the captains of this industry felt compelled to acknowledge
the arguments of its detractors. That's when Tony Aitken, an
executive vice-president of Inco, assured the Canadian Institute of Mining and Metallurgy that '[t]he 1990s is going to be
the decade of the environment, and by the time the year 2000
comes, all of us will be committed environmentalists, like it or
not, because the problems are real'. Aitken went on to describe
public perceptions of miners as 'people who work holes in the
ground. [The public] think of open pits. They think of blowing
dust, they think of smoke emissions, they think of deserted towns
and scarred landscapes, they think of everything that is negative
in terms of our environmental impacts. Let's acknowledge the
reality of that.'[3]

One reality was that, over the following ten years, Aitken's own
company was to hold on to its unenviable position as Canada's
biggest belcher of sulphur dioxide emissions. Other North American companies didn't fare much better: in 2002, plants operated

by Kennecott Copper (absorbed by Rio Tinto in 1997) were cited by the US Environmental Protection Agency as the first, thirteenth and nineteenth greatest toxic polluters in the entire USA.[4]

As the 'green decade' wore on, it became clear that much more than propitiatory rhetoric was required. Miners were becoming mired in one credibility crisis after another. First came the rebellion against Rio Tinto's Bougainville copper-gold mine in 1989, which forced the company to withdraw from the island under a hail of bullets. Not long afterwards, Yonggom people living in the Star mountains of Papua New Guinea, outraged at pollution from BHPBilliton's Ok Tedi operations, mounted blockades against the company – 'to bougainville', as they dubbed it. In 1995 an unprecedented global campaign was launched to bring Freeport and Rio Tinto to account for the unexampled devastation and militarization their Grasberg operations had brought to the Amungme and Komoro peoples of West Papua.[5] John Bray of Control Risks himself acknowledged that international protests against human rights and environmental violations around the Grasberg mine became 'as much a part of the mine's political risk profile as Amungme [local] tribespeople'.[6] A year later, the Yonggom secured US$28.6 million in damages from BHPBilliton, after bringing a case for 'negligence resulting in loss of amenity' due to the company's poisoning of the Ok Tedi and Fly river systems.[7]

Galloping exploitation of finite resources was increasingly being characterized by development and environmental NGOs as the antithesis of sustainable development. Almost every new foray into virgin territory, particularly in Latin America, South and South East Asia, triggered massive community opposition. Most of it came from indigenous and tribal peoples, some of whom felt they might finally be close to securing formal recognition of their right to determine the use of minerals beneath their lands. The ILO Convention (no. 169), concerning Indigenous and Tribal Peoples in Independent Countries, had entered into force on 5

September 1991. While it fell considerably short of the demands then being framed by the United Nations Working Group on Indigenous Populations, it would nevertheless be invoked on several occasions in the years to come.[8]

By the dawn of the twenty-first century, most untapped gold, copper, iron, bauxite, nickel and diamonds had been identified as effectively indigenous 'property'.[9] Worse, from the industry's point of view, the price of many key metals had been dramatically falling, while costs of extraction were inexorably rising.

Globalizing the propaganda

The industry solution was eventually to be the Global Mining Initiative (GMI) of 1999. The ground for this had been prepared six years earlier, in a behind-the-scenes ploy to snatch a reasonably promising draft code of corporate conduct from the jaws of the UN Centre for Transnational Corporations (UNCTC). Initially the code was welcomed by a large number of South-based states, which regarded it as key tool to conserve their resource endowment and reclaim their trading rights.[10] But, as pointed out by Desiree Abrahams of the UN Research Institute for Social Development (UNRISD), by the time it was close to being finalized, many of these countries had already succumbed to 'neo liberal ideology'.[11] For multinationals the proposal had always been the proverbial 'red rag to a bull', and work on the code was abandoned just before the Rio de Janeiro World Summit on Sustainable Development (WSSD) in 1992.

> Sidestepping the UNCTC's proposal at the Summit, the Business Council for Sustainable Development (BCSD) together with the International Chamber of Commerce (ICC) presented voluntary corporate self-regulation. This proposition received an official seal of approval and consequently, with its *raison d'être* destroyed, it was only a matter of time until the UNCTC was disbanded in 1993.[12]

Four years later, in 1997, the BCSD merged with the World Industry Council for the Environment (WICE) to form the World Business Council for Sustainable Development (WBCSD), in which heads of extractive industry were soon to play leading roles. Steering the WBCSD was Stephan Schmidheiny (he had also set up the BCSD), supported by his close friend Maurice Strong, the secretary-general of the Rio Summit. Strong was big in Canadian oil, and Schmidheiny was a scion of the family that ran Holcim, the global asbestos and cement producer (see Chapter 5).

It became clear that, on its own, this broad initiative could not cope with steadily mounting, well-documented accusations made against the hard rock mining industry, and high-profile mining multinationals in particular. A few companies had already managed to engage some NGOs in 'dialogues', and in 1996 Rio Tinto scored a minor coup by recruiting well-known environmentalist Tom Burke (a former executive director of Friends of the Earth UK) as a special adviser. But such gambits convinced few, including the media. Urgently needed was a new project to deflect growing public alarm. It should appear innovative, inclusive and committed, but without making too many hard commitments. Above all, it must divert attention away from specific corporate misdeeds by involving the industry per se in civil discourses about sustainability and corporate social responsibility. Thus, in early 1999 at Davos – just as the World Economic Forum was under siege from various peoples' movements – Rio Tinto's chairman, Robert Wilson, delivered his package in the shape of the Global Mining Initiative (GMI), soon to be endorsed by eight other global mining multinationals.[13] It was surely no coincidence that Davos was also chosen by UN Secretary-General Kofi Annan for the launching of his Global Compact 'to bring companies together with UN Agencies, labour and civil society, to support universal environmental and social principles'. This, too, was a project in which Rio Tinto participated from the outset.

The GMI mapped out a three-stage strategy. First, there would be a major research endeavour under 'neutral' auspices, to 'examine the relationship between the world's minerals system and the goal of sustainable development', called Mining, Minerals and Sustainable Development (MMSD). Following this a new industry body would be established called the International Council on Mining and Metals (ICMM). Then, mining's core leadership would descend on the second World Summit for Sustainable Development (WSSD), scheduled for late August 2002 in Johannesburg.

Mining, minerals and sustainable development

'The truth is that sustainability means quite different things depending which side of the bulldozer you are on.'[14]

The MMSD became possibly the most detailed dissection of a single industrial sector ever undertaken. Initially under the aegis of the WBCSD, the project was later contracted to the London-based International Institute for Environment and Development (IIED) and put into the hands of Luke Danielson, who had considerable experience working with NGOs.[15] The study cost several million pounds, mainly subscribed by thirty mining companies. It benefited from twenty submissions by 'multi-stakeholder' and expert workshops as well as another 100 background and research reports. Conspicuous by their absence from the process were most of the groups whose claims and grievances lay at the root of the malaise that the MMSD was supposed to address. Some NGOs were invited to join in its early days but not the majority of critical community and indigenous organizations. None of them was asked to help frame the MMSD protocols. One major weakness of the whole exercise (I view it as a fatal flaw) lay in the fact that the MMSD was destined to wind up precisely at the point where it might have handed further deliberations over to a truly independent forum. But then there was never any intention that it should achieve a life of its own. From the outset, the stakeholders of the GMI determined that the MMSD would effectively fall on its own sword while its own industry body, the ICMM, emerged centre-stage.

The MMSD's final report was entitled *Breaking New Ground*.[16] In truth, it did little more than gather up a large and disparate scattering of existing opinions, many of considerable interest, but failing to gel into a clear programme which could be widely comprehended and endorsed. Three months after its publication, Sir Mark Moody-Stuart, the new chair of Anglo American, and Lord Richard Holme (who had recently retired from Rio Tinto), flew shoulder to shoulder with the British prime minister and his International Development Secretary, Clare Short, to Johannesburg for the second World Summit on Sustainable Development. Just as at the first event in Rio de Janeiro, ten years earlier, much of the ideological ground for this one was prepared by the WBCSD. It had already joined with the ICC in establishing Business Action for Sustainable Development (BASD), which appointed Moody-Stuart as its chairman, with Lord Holme riding shotgun as his 'adviser'. According to Moody-Stuart BASD was designed to 'ensure that the world business community is assigned its proper place at the summit and its preparations, and that we are seen to be playing a progressive and constructive role, with a business-like emphasis on action and an openness to partnership'.[17]

Three weeks before the summit – the largest-ever event of its kind – the London *Financial Times* offered its opinion that, since 'Sir Mark is credited with the recovery of Shell's image in the aftermath of its mid-1990's difficulties he is regarded as highly credible by environmental and social groups'.[18] That judgement was ludicrously wide of the mark. It could not be denied, however, that Moody-Stuart and Holme, solidly backed by the UK government at the WSSD, were to act as the most powerful advocates of so-called 'Type Two' partnerships between government, civil society and companies – even while banging the drum for their respective companies. Although the Liberal Democrat Lord Holme soon dropped from the UK public eye (he was severely criticized by left-wingers within his own party for his relationship with Rio Tinto), Moody-Stuart went on to become a key adviser to the World Bank's *Extractive Industries Review* (see Chapter 2). And, in 2006, still at the helm of Anglo American, he was promoted to chairman of the Foundation for the UN Global Compact.

Through the past decade and a half the minerals industry has travelled from the back-seat role it adopted at Rio in 1992, via the unique GMI process, to seeing its leadership now at the helm of global processes defining sustainability and corporate social responsibility. Even its staunchest critics must admit that it has been a remarkably successful journey. How did practitioners of 'everything that is negative in terms of our environmental impacts' (to quote Inco's Tony Aitken back in 1989) turn perceptions around so dramatically, even while their bad practices were, if anything, becoming worse? There is no pat answer to this, but I offer a few conjectures. Unlike Big Oil, which has been brazen in its sponsorship of self-exculpatory pseudo-scientific studies purporting to refute evidence of adverse climate change, Big Mining's MMSD study was genuinely objective. Wary of blundering into global forums on sustainability simply wearing their own hats, Wilson, Moody-Stuart and Schmidheiny gradually unfolded their road map through bigger, more objective-sounding initiatives; not only the Global Compact but also the Extractive Industries Transparency Initiative, announced by UK prime minister Blair at the 2002 WSSD. In the wake of this second world summit, their corporate representatives also assiduously participated in the post-Rio Agenda 21 plan of action, attended meetings of the UN Working Group on Indigenous Populations, and enthusiastically backed the Kimberley Process, aimed at banning 'conflict' diamonds.

As with other industrial sectors that are suffering a tarnished image, mining companies purchase the services of professionals, who now include economists, anthropologists and ex-diplomats. One of the latter is Richard Ralph, British ambassador to Lima from 2003 to 2006. In late 2005, Ralph vigorously defended UK-listed Monterrico Metals from claims that it had been behind armed attacks on opponents living close to a planned copper mine in north-west Peru.[19] For his loyalty, Ralph was rewarded by being appointed chairman of the company. Equally productive has been Big Mining's infiltration of scientific institutions and, in one case, the sponsoring of an entire university (see Box 7.1). The ploy not only seeks to insert extractive industry within the broad stream of academic discourse, but also to recruit blue- and white-collar staff for its own purposes. Most important, however, have been two carefully honed strategies directed at the biggest civil society challenges that miners currently face. The first is aimed at persuading major environmental and development NGOs that collaboration in 'partnerships' will benefit them both, and it has achieved a remarkable degree of success. The second tries to frame the vexatious question of participation in negotiations for a mineral lease in terms of legitimization through a 'multi-stakeholder' process. So far, this strategy has failed to meet with widespread acceptance – but for how much longer?

Taking one's partners

In 1992, CARE sponsored a 'resettlement programme' in Sierra Leone together with the North American miner Sierra Rutile. At the time this was a relatively isolated example of NGO coopera-tion with a mining company, then the world's biggest supplier of titanium oxide from mineral sands. CARE lent its field support

to a specific 'development objective' – providing better sanitation, healthcare, housing, economic opportunities, education
and income generation for 5,300 people who had been ejected
from reasonably fertile land. A report published by Friends of
the Earth (UK) in 1997, however, concluded that, despite some
improvements in living standards, the regeneration scheme had
failed on several counts: the resource base had been severely
reduced and the public health programme received 'minimal'
lack of community participation, thus posing 'a very real issue,
and little has been done to resolve it'.[20]

Seven years later, both the pace and the nature of Big NGO–corporate mining partnerships had markedly changed. These were
no longer confined to discrete ventures in one country, but began
to involve wide-ranging organizational endorsements of company
policies. Soon the distinction between independent charitable endeavour and corporate profit-making became distinctly blurred,
and on occasion it has disappeared altogether. In a major 2004
critique of the US NGO Conservation International (CI) and the
World Wide Fund for Nature (WWF), Worldwatch's Marc Chapin
analysed this disturbing dialectic. Between 1990 and 1996, says
Chapin, the big environmental NGOs seemed to be taking their
lead from indigenous communities. For example, the 1990 Declaration of Iquitos had pledged several environmental NGOs (including, later, the International Union for the Conservation of
Nature, IUCN) to 'continue working in the future as an alliance
of indigenous peoples and environmentalists for an Amazonia
for humanity'. Six years later, a set of Principles and Guidelines
on Indigenous and Traditional Peoples and Protected Areas was
signed with apparent unanimity between these community organizations and the NGOs. But this unity was soon displaced 'by talk
of changed priorities, with a new focus on large-scale conservation strategies and the importance of science, rather than social
realities, in determining their agendas'. A bandwagon had been

drawn up, on to which many organizations would jump, throwing up initiatives variously called 'community-based natural resource management', 'community-based conservation', 'sustainable development and use', 'grassroots conservation', 'devolution of resource rights to local communities' and 'integrated conservation and development programmes' (ICDPs). According to Chapin:

Conservationist agendas often begin with the need to establish protected areas that are off limits to people, and to develop management plans. If they include indigenous peoples in their plans, they tend to see those peoples more as a possible means to an end rather than as ends in themselves. They are seldom willing to support legal battles over land tenure and the strengthening of indigenous organizations; they consider these actions 'too political' and outside their conservationist mandate. They have been reluctant to support indigenous peoples in their struggles against oil, mining, and logging companies that are destroying vast swathes of rainforest throughout the world. Again, the excuse is that such interventions would be 'too political', and the conservationists often defer to national governments to handle those matters. ... Each of the large conservation NGOs has close financial and political ties to the governments, bilateral and multilateral agencies, and multinational corporations operating throughout the Third World, and is reluctant to oppose them.

Concludes Chapin: ' This has given rise to the ironic observation that the large international NGOs are allying themselves with forces that are destroying the world's remaining ecosystems, while ignoring or even opposing those forces that are attempting to save them from destruction.'[21] I leave the reader to judge to what extent Chapin's analysis is confirmed, by examining the following examples (by no means exhaustive) of such alliances:

1996: WWF-Canada threatens to sue the Canadian federal govern-

ment for approving Canada's first diamond mine (to be operated by BHPBilliton), without designating protected areas for
the central Arctic region. But WWF then withdraws its lawsuit
in return for a government commitment to develop a Northwest
Territories Protected Areas Strategy. Since that strategy was approved in 1999, allegedly WWF has not formally identified, much
less established, any protected areas in the central Arctic, while
only two areas have received temporary protection elsewhere in
the Northwest Territories.[22]

1998–2001: CARE (UK), the UK Department for International
Development and the World Bank set up and manage the mining component of the Business Partners for Development Programme. Only two out of the seven projects 'adopted' are later
considered by the accountancy firm PricewaterhouseCoopers to
meet criteria for successful 'tri sector partnership'. One of the
projects is withdrawn from the World Bank/IFC's portfolio for not
meeting World Bank performance standards (see Chapter 2).

1999–present: US-based Human Rights Watch and Amnesty International draw up a code of human rights principles for Freeport-Rio Tinto at its Grasberg mine in West Papua. The code
fails to recognize indigenous rights to the area, which has been
exploited by the mining company since the 1970s; or mounting
opposition on the part of West Papuan independence fighters
and students to the company's presence in the territory. Although
the agreement pledges Freeport not to employ the Indonesian
armed forces to protect its interests, it says nothing about the
company's cooperation with the army (for example, by their funding of the construction of a military barracks). Over the following
six years, the company continues to make major contributions
directly to the army.[23] To its credit Human Rights Watch has
continued criticizing the company and exposing the abuse of
human rights in West Papua.

2000–present: The World Conservation Union (IUCN) and the International Council on Mining and Metals (ICMM) agree that, once companies have secured an exploration licence in World Heritage sites, they should be allowed to develop any economic mineral deposit under certain conditions.[24] Shortly afterwards, IUCN refuses to come out in opposition to Rio Tinto's threat to exploit the Jabiluka uranium deposit, located in a designated World Heritage site in northern Australia. Several prominent indigenous peoples' organizations and mining-affected communities jointly decry the partnership. Tom Goldtooth of the Indigenous Environmental Networks declares it to be 'a contradiction for the ICMM, whose mining industry members have systematically engaged in the rape of the Mother Earth to have suddenly changed heart to implement best management practices to protect biodiversity. By nature of its technology, mining is unsustainable.'[25] The furore caused by the announcement forces the IUCN to modify its stance, henceforth referring to 'consultation' rather than 'collaboration'. Nevertheless, the ICMM continues to refer to IUCN as a 'partner'.

2000–present: Lafarge-Blue Circle, the world's dominant cement manufacturer, shells out £3.5 million to WWF in order to become a 'Conservation partner' (*sic*) to the world's best-known environmental organization. WWF then undertakes assessments of the company's reductions in global greenhouse gas emissions. WWF has to date said almost nothing about the effect of Lafarge's mining methods on people in countries such as India and the Philippines. It kept largely silent about the company's proposal for a super-quarry on the Scottish isle of Harris in 2003, until the outcry from other environmental groups forced it belatedly to join the chorus (see also Chapter 5).

2001–present: BirdLife International launches the 'Birds and the Environment' programme with Rio Tinto, claiming that the

partnership is 'fuelled by mutually held objectives of integrat-
ing biodiversity conservation into core business practices'. In
2004, the charity announces that it has protected nearly 170,000
hectares of a new National Park on the Indonesian island of Hal-
mahera. This is also home, however, to a major proposed nickel
mine to be operated by Canadian-based Weda Bay Minerals in
an area ostensibly protected by the nation's 1999 Forest Protection Act.[26]

2001–present: Conservation International accepts funding from
Rio Tinto to critique its environmental and social impact assessment for a massive titanium strip mine in south-eastern Madagascar. Conservation International,[27] WWF and Friends of the
Earth (UK) (FOE) all find major defects in the scheme. By 2005
Rio Tinto has modified some aspects of its mine plan, but FOE
continues to oppose the project, on both social and ecological
grounds. But both CI and WWF drop their objections.

2001–present: The Eden project – now Britain's most successful
tourist attraction – is established on a worked-out china clay
quarry in the south-west county of Cornwall by a newly consti-
tuted UK civil society organization and Rio Tinto. In 2004 the
project is expanded to include a post-mine regeneration centre,
with the additional sponsorship of Anglo American and English
Nature.[28]

2002–2003: WWF International takes umbrage at US aluminium
giant Alcoa's plan to dam 22 square miles of glacial territory in
Iceland, in order to capture hydro-power for a future smelter.
Alcoa in the meantime has gained membership of WWF-USA's
'corporate club' by paying a minimum of US$1 million, while
Kathryn Fuller, president of WWF-USA, has accepted an offer
to join Alcoa's board.[29]

2003: Greeted with considerable scepticism, WWF announces an offer to certify 'good' mines, along the lines of the Forest Steward-ship Council and its marine equivalent[30] (see Chapter 8).

2004: WWF and RMC Austria sign an agreement to protect a rare Austrian grassland, designated in 1999 as an international Biogenetic Reserve. The aim is to upgrade the 'ecological value' of RMC's Hollitzer Quarry – although the mine operates next to the reserve.[31]

2004–2005: Oxfam-Community Aid Abroad (CAA), based in Aus-tralia, invites ten BHPBilliton upper-echelon employees to join its Corporate Community Leadership Programme (CCLP) in Orissa, India. The aim is to show company representatives best examples of development work, for them to discover 'the negative impact that poorly managed minerals operations can have on impoverished communities', and 'to improve their community dialogue technique with community groups'.[32] BHPBilliton has already signalled its intention to seek exploration leases in the state, and the Indian national advocacy organization mines, min-erals and People (mmP) refuses to participate in the programme. Following severe criticism from community organizations – and late in the day – those groups that opted to engage with the company withdraw from the process. BHPBilliton goes on to secure rights to a huge bauxite deposit adjacent to the Karlapat wildlife sanctuary.

2006: One of the most contentious corporate deals ever brokered by WWF is also one of the most recent. In 2004, WWF-Canada's Monte Hummel had 'traded places' with his opposite number, Scott Hand of Inco, to become 'CEOs for a day'.[33] Two years later, the conservation organization and the world's second-largest nickel miner sign up to an alliance. By then, WWF-Canada is fully aware that Inco has consistently been indicted as the largest polluter among Canadian miners. In March 2006, the FTSE4Good

company index, set up by the *Financial Times* to monitor compliance with certain business standards, throws out Inco for
'not meeting Human Rights Criteria'.[34] Inco is the only mining
company ever to be deleted from the FTSE4Good index on these
grounds. Yet, just seven months later, WWF-Canada accepts from
Inco a million Canadian dollars, spread over the next five years,
in order to 'advance a number of conservation initiatives'. The
organization says it has 'a track record of engaging with companies to reduce their ecological footprint' and works 'with big
industry, like mining and forestry, because it is vital to achieve
our conservation goals. Expanding our relationship with Inco is a
logical and welcome next step for us both. We are excited about
what we can accomplish together.'[35] The ink is still wet on the
agreement when Inco is blockaded by thousands of indigenous
citizens of Goro in New Caledonia, trying desperately to halt
Inco's illegal construction of one of the world's biggest nickel-
cobalt mines. The indigenous peoples' organization Rheebu Nuu
had campaigned against the project for five years. It claims that
Inco failed to carry out a valid environmental impact study on
a vast open-pit project. As a result 10,000 tonnes of dissolved
metals a year would spew into the ocean; while manganese contamination was likely to reach 100mg/litre of water – a hundred
times the level allowed in metropolitan France. On 21 October
2006, a Parisian court rules that Inco (by then merged with CVRD
of Brazil) must stop construction or face a daily penalty.

Box 7.1 *Digging the fields of academe*

Mining companies have been endowing universities, estab-
lishing chairs and financing scholarships for many years.
Notable among them is Rio Tinto which funds Imperial
College in London, one of the top engineering universities

anywhere. The degree to which Jim-Bob Moffett, chair of Freeport, has personally infiltrated Louisiana State University (LSU) has provoked widespread campus protests for a decade. Both LSU and the University of Texas at Austin have accepted extensive donations from Freeport, including a named professorship at LSU.

Back in the eighties, CRA (now Rio Tinto Ltd) created a stink at Monash University, Melbourne, by purchasing part of its property for a technology centre. Inco sponsors university buildings in Canada as well as having representatives on several boards of regents and governors. Not content with dishing out a substantial amount to establish Dundee University's Centre of Energy, Petroleum, Mineral Law and Policy (CEPMLP – the leading 'think tank' implementing revisions to state mining codes), Rio Tinto also headhunts candidates to do the centre's work. Despite the posturing of a 'tripartite' process between the CEPMLP, the company and the British Foreign and Commonwealth Office, by its own admission Rio Tinto makes the final decision on awarding the scholarships.

In India, the iron and steel producer Tata Group has endowed four 'great and good temples of learning' (to borrow its own description), including the well-reputed Institute of Social Science and the JRD Tata Ecotechnology Centre. Yet, however valuable or academically objective the research flowing from these temples may be, the results rarely 'trickle down' to Tata's operations on the ground. This was graphically demonstrated by the company's complicity in the Kalinganagar massacre of 2 January 2006, when it allowed (even if it didn't instruct) police to murder twelve protesters against a planned steel plant. Another Indian magnate, the executive chairman of Vedanta Resources plc, is going a big step farther. Anil Agarwal intends to establish an eponymous university to 'nurture tomorrow's Nobel Laureates, Olympic champions and community leaders'. He hopes to have the university launched in mid-2008 on a plot near the eastern coast of Orissa, adjacent to several sites of high biodiversity and of spiritual significance.

The US private consultancy A. T. Kearney is assisting Vedanta in achieving its further-learning aims; and Kearney is a force to be reckoned with. It set up the Global Business Policy Council to promote globalization, with an elite of world CEOs, is also closely associated with the US *Foreign Policy* magazine and claims to be regarded by British Petroleum (BP) as its 'corporate policy' consultant.[36]

When decisions are at stake

One of the greatest triumphs of the minerals industry in appropriating both language and intellectual space has been its recuperation of putative opponents as so-called 'stakeholders'. The term 'multi-stakeholder' confers an aura of integrity on negotiations, reassuring sceptics that they are not alone in potentially fraught negotiations with a company. Many civil society groups now uncritically use the term and are thereby, at least partly, bound by its formalities of discourse. Although the idea may not have been born within the mining sector, resource extraction companies zealously cherish it, clearly believing that several nagging problems may be mitigated at a single stroke. Community leaders who refuse, on principle, to sit down and talk with corporate representatives are subtly disenfranchised, not just from company-sponsored discussions but from wider public debate. In contrast, the methods employed by the company to secure its own 'stake' – however illegitimate or contingent on bribery and coercion they may be – tend to get overlooked. In 1997 Rio Tinto hosted several public forums in southern Mindanao, the Philippines, under the aegis of its chief anthropologist, Glyn Cochrane. The main dissent to the company's exploration plans came from the indigenous Subaanen, many of whom refused to participate in discussions, declaring that they knew the damage mining would cause and therefore rejected it on principle. The forums proceeded nevertheless. On their conclusion Rio Tinto seemed satisfied that it had gained a 'social licence to operate'. Subaanen opposition was not quelled, however, and by then they were backed by a significant number of international supporters. The company decided to send out an independent US anthropologist, Charles Frake, to further canvass the community's views. Following submission of Frake's report, Rio Tinto chairman Robert Wilson claimed that Frake had confirmed the majority of Subaanen to be behind the proposed exploration. In fact (as revealed in a private letter)[37] Frake had told the company that he was unable to determine what the community's opinions were.

Primary resource holders (custodians) who do join such forums are allocated a place, just like any other, at the bargaining table, even though they stand to lose most from any resource use agreement. They may end up being given a derisory share of the outcome in the form of compensation or benefits packages. But rarely will they be recognized as the negotiator *primus inter pares*. Conversely, those (especially Northern environmental NGOs) who collaborate with a company are treated as if they were bona fide decision-makers, even though they may lack authority from local people.

Dayak villagers, forcibly removed from the Kelian gold mine site in the Indonesian province of East Kalimantan, finally secured a compensation package that satisfied some of them (though by no means all). Their representative organization,

Winning hearts and mines

LKMTL, however, was given no pre-emptive place on the Mine Closure Steering Committee, established to settle numerous outstanding environmental issues before Rio Tinto, the mine operator, was due to quit the scene. LKMTL had repeatedly asked that Rio Tinto take responsibility for the long-term environmental security and protection of the community's health and livelihoods. Their demands included independent environmental monitoring and free hospital facilities. When Rio Tinto refused to entertain these demands, LKMTL withdrew from the Mine Closure Steering Committee and Working Groups in 2003, 'because it felt the committee was only a token gesture and did not take community concerns and solutions seriously'. Later, however, 'its representatives were forced to return by [the mine's] management who threatened to withhold payments promised to the community organisation'.[38]

Defining 'community'

In theory, any party claiming to be potentially affected by the impacts of a mining venture may put themselves forward as a stakeholder. In practice, it is local people who have most difficulty getting 'authenticated'. At the root of this anomaly is the definition of 'community'. Although a government may not recognize villagers' pre-existing land and subsoil rights, nowadays many mining companies invite representatives to consultations, afraid that exclusion will lead to unwelcome community agitation and materially delay their project. The social researcher Paul Kapelus has made a detailed examination of how one such company (Rio Tinto again) selected its preferred partners for a negotiating exercise in South Africa over expansion of its Richard's Bay Minerals (RBM) titanium mine. Even where principles and guidelines were apparently implemented, says Kapelus, Rio Tinto was continually assessing its current or future profits against the consequences of including, or marginalizing, certain groups. 'In situations where the costs of being socially responsible do not help keep total costs down, then local managers will have to confront the tension between being socially responsible and the demand to increase (enhance) shareholder value.' These managers will always want to find (or appear to find) some way to ease this tension. 'Probably the most effective method ... is to shape the definition of the community in ways that restrict the number of claims upon them as a business enterprise. ... This is a means by which firms limit costs ...'[39]

'Legitimacy' in negotiations with the company inevitably becomes assigned to those individuals still left 'at the table', even though they may no longer represent the views of those who have already left. Once a 'legitimate' local partner has been identified then the firm's plans can proceed in a smoother manner (and responses to any objections from dissenters can be more effectively developed and implemented). The tendency is

> to designate local (economic and traditional) elites as the legitimate authorities in the community. ... Typically, it would not be in the interests of firms to raise the question of the criteria by which such authorities could be considered legitimate. Nor is it generally in their interests to note any disagreements within the community (unless the dissenters can impose significant costs), as this may undermine the legitimacy of the leaders of the community and the firm's claim to be socially responsible.

On the surface, Rio Tinto seems to allow for a broad understanding of community and a diversity of forms of community. The former characteristic is indicated in its definition of 'community' as 'anyone who is impacted in any way, socially, economically and environmentally by the operations of the mine'. The company is keen to recognize a wide variety of possible bases for communities, including 'the nature of attachment to a territory; self identification by others as members of a distinct group; the culture or common beliefs, attitudes and work interests of the group; a language or dialect, which may be different from the national language; the presence of unique religious, political or cultural beliefs'.

However, says Kapelus,

> In other places ... [Rio Tinto's] documents suggest a narrower understanding of community and more limited responsibilities. Thus, for example, when the company proclaims its commitment to protecting the dignity, well-being and rights of people with whom they are 'directly' involved, it identifies these people as employees and their families, and people in 'neighbouring' communities. The ambiguity over community in the documents makes it unclear whether the firm views CSR primarily in terms of moral responsibility or business strategy. The fact that there might be a tension between these two approaches is never addressed. Rather the firm seems to assume a harmony between its moral responsibilities and its business interests.

Concludes Kapelus:

> In the case of RBM ... we have seen how a Rio Tinto subsidiary adopts a notion of community that tends to restrict the firm's obligations. In terms of boundaries ... RBM defines the community as the [localized] MTA rather that the larger sub-district or district in which it operates. In terms of structure, RBM tends to make simplifying assumptions about the community (e.g. that the local authority is legitimate, that there are no significant conflicts of interests, etc.) ... These assumptions about the nature of the community serve to reduce RBM's costs (by allowing them to streamline decision-making, not take into account certain issues and claims, etc.).
>
> ... It is ... possible to acknowledge that the community is at times divided by different interests, values and strategies. This is the approach that is taken by the various opponents of Rio Tinto.

Doing so, however, is likely to increase the demands on RBM and Rio Tinto and, thereby, increase their costs (and decrease profits).[40]

Put bluntly, money remains the cold bottom line whatever the rhetoric or devices used to distract from that objective. In this instance Kapelus implicitly identified a 'critical mass' against Rio Tinto; one which knows that its communities do exist and that they pre-date, and should preclude, any external intervention seeking to limit their self-definition.

Not only for Rio Tinto, but for almost every other large mining company, that's a bridge which is far too far.

Notes

1 A. Carey, *Taking the Risk out of Democracy: Corporate Propaganda versus Freedom and Liberty*, University of Illinois Press, 1997.

2 Quoted in A. Rowell, 'Dialogue or deception?', *DELTA*, Newsletter of the Ogoni Support Group in Britain, no. 4, 1999.

3 K. Gooding, 'Preparing for the green decade', *Financial Times*, London, 2 October 1989.

4 Environmental Protection Agency (EPA), 'Toxic Release Inventory 2002', 2003.

5 The campaign is well documented in A. Gedicks, *Resource Rebels: Native Challenges to Mining and Oil Corporations*, South End Press, Cambridge, MA, 2001, pp. 91–126.

6 J. Bray, 'No hiding place: business and the politics of pressure', Control Risks Group, London, 1997, p. 45.

7 S. Kirsch, *Reverse Anthropology: Indigenous Analysis of Social and Environmental Relations in New Guinea*, Stanford University Press, Stanford, CA, 2006, p. 41.

8 Article 15 of ILO Convention 169 guarantees a 'special safeguard' for 'natural resources pertaining to [indigenous] lands', but only in so far as they 'include the right ... to participate in the use, management and conservation of these resources'. Where the state 'retains the ownership of mineral or sub-surface resources or rights to other resources pertaining to lands' (in practice virtually every state), governments 'shall establish or maintain procedures through which they shall consult these peoples, with a view to ascertaining whether and to what degree their interests would be prejudiced, before undertaking or permitting any programmes for the exploration or exploitation ... ' In practice this

is no more than the World Bank affirmed twelve years later, following its own Extractive Industries Review. Article 16 appears to establish the principle of 'free prior informed consent (FPIC)' before indigenous communities may be uprooted from their territory. What is given by one clause is, however, ripped away in another that is hedged about with ambiguities: 'Where their consent cannot be obtained, such relocation shall take place only following *appropriate procedures* established by national laws and regulations, including public inquiries *where appropriate*, which provide the *opportunity* for effective representation of the peoples concerned [my italics].'

9 In 1996 I carried out a study for the World Council of Churches' Consultation on Mining and Indigenous Peoples, which attempted to identify the geographical location of key economic reserves of various metals around the world. These were then matched with the boundaries of areas of indigenous peoples' occupation, or to which indigenous communities have a compelling claim. Although this study has not been updated since, I have little doubt that the proportion of such territory, currently targeted by mining companies, has, if anything, increased.

10 D. Abrahams, *Regulations for Corporations: an Historical Account of TNC Regulations*, UNRISD, Geneva, 2005, p. 5.

11 Ibid., p. 6.

12 Ibid., p. 7.

13 According to Luke Danielson, project director of the MMSD, a critical element of the GMI enterprise was 'the very visible backing and authority provided by Rio Tinto's chairman and other visible industry leaders and the demonstration effect this had for other company CEO's'. See L. Danielson, *Architecture for Change: an Account of the Mining, Minerals and Sustainable Development Project: History*, Global Public Policy Institute, Berlin, 2006, p. 19.

14 A. Whitmore, 'The emperor's new clothes: sustainable mining?', *Journal of Cleaner Production*, 2006, 14(3–4): 309.

15 Danielson, 'Architecture for change', p. 20.

16 *Breaking New Ground: Mining, Minerals, and Sustainable Development, the Report of the MMSD Project*, Earthscan, London, 2002.

17 Moody-Stuart was quoted by Jack Whelan of the International Chamber of Commerce in ICC's 'Statement by business and industry to the 10th Session, UN Commission on Sustainable Development', 30 April 2001.

18 *Financial Times*, London, 17 July 2002.

19 'Grave attacks carried out by Monterrico Metals and Minera Majaz against campesinos in the Hormiguero, Carmen de La Frontera District, Huancababa Provience, Peru', Press release by the Front for the

Sustainable Development of the Northern Frontier of Perú, 3 November 2006.

20 S. Kamara (ed. T. Rice), *Mined Out: the Environmental and Social Implications of Development Finance of Rutile Mining in Sierra Leone*, Friends of the Earth (UK), 1997, pp. 31–4.

21 M. Chapin, 'A challenge to conservationists', excerpted from the November/December 2004 *Worldwatch* magazine.

22 P. Cisek, 'Scouring scum and tar from the bottom of the pit', *Canadian Dimension* magazine, July/August 2006.

23 See 'Paying for protection: the Freeport mine and the Indonesian security forces', Global Witness, London, 2005.

24 B. Burton in *Mining Monitor*, MPI, Sydney, March 2001; see also 'Report on the technical workshop on world heritage and mining', IUCN HQ, Gland, 21–23 September 2000.

25 'Statement issued by Tebtebba Foundation, African Indigenous Women's Organisation, Indigenous Information Network, Asian Indigenous Women's Network, International Indian Treaty Council Indigenous Women's Network, Third World Network et al.', 2002

26 Environment News Service, USA, 11 November 2004.

27 'Review of an ilmenite mining project in South East Madagascar', Conservation International, October 2001.

28 *Mining Environmental Management*, January 2004.

29 Nostromo Research, 'London calling', Mines and Communities website, 19 February 2003.

30 B. Burton, 'Trading credibility – accreditation scheme for good mines meets with community distrust', *New Internationalist*, April 2003.

31 *Mining Environmental Management*, January 2004, p. 4.

32 BHPBilliton Health, Safety, Environment & Community Report, 2004.

33 A. Maitland, 'The benefits of trading places', *Financial Times*, 26 July 2004.

34 'Semi-annual review of the FTSE4Good indices', *Financial Times*, London, March 2006.

35 Inco Ltd, 'News release: Inco and WWF-Canada announce $1 million conservation program', 3 October 2006.

36 'London calling', Mines and Communities website, London, 20 February 2006.

37 This is the text of the letter by Charles O. Frake, Samuel P. Capen Professor of Anthropology at the University of Buffalo State, University of New York, sent on 6 March 1998 to Frank Nally, SSC, of the Columban Missionary Society: 'Thank you for your communication. I share your concern for the welfare of the Subaanen people. What follows is a full copy of the only written report I submitted to Rio Tinto [notes

withheld]. They did not ask for recommendations and I offered none. They have not asked for any written elaboration of the topics I listed. Also at no time have I ever presumed to advocate a position to the Sub-aanen on this or any other issue. Sincerely, Charles Frake.'

38 'Rio Tinto closes Kelian mine – history of human rights abuses', *Down to Earth*, 65, May 2005.

39 P. Kapelus, 'Mining, corporate social responsibility and the "community": the case of Rio Tinto, Richard's Bay Minerals and the Mbonambi', *Journal of Business Ethics*, 2002, 39: 275–96.

40 Ibid.

8 | No means no!

My previous chapter traced how the minerals industry, though widely disparaged a mere decade ago as destructive, dirty and dangerous, has come to persuade a significant section of civil society that it is now the opposite. Yet it confronts opposition, more vehement than ever before, precisely from those supposed to benefit most from its conversion to corporate social responsibility and sustainable development goals. Surely this is evidence enough that, when supping with this particular 'devil', no spoon can be too long? The collaboration of certain NGOs with big miners is all the more baffling, considering that companies consistently fail to meet even their own weak performance standards or to implement safe technologies. However, the 1999–2002 Global Mining Initiative (GMI) was never intended to tie miners down to mandatory oversight of their operations. The International Council on Mining and Metals (ICMM)'s 'ten principles' were studiously framed so that miners could avoid being bound by their objectives. They include an ephemeral 'goal' to 'minimise involuntary resettlement', without defining the term; and to 'respect the culture and heritage of local communities, including Indigenous Peoples', while strenuously resisting implementation of community-controlled 'fully informed prior consent'. The ICMM also has signally failed to reject the practices of riverine and submarine tailings disposal (STD), despite their transparent violation of the precautionary principle. It is true that in 2003 the Council did frown upon encroachment within biosphere reserves and other protected sites. But by then some of its most influential members, including BHPBilliton, Inco and Rio Tinto, had chipped away at Indonesia's 1999 Forestry Act to avoid surrendering leases over twenty-two such sanctuaries.[1] And just last year the New York-based International Network for Economic, Social and Cultural Rights (ESCR), Global Witness, Amnesty International and the UK-based Rights and Account-ability in Development (RAID) cited a dozen mining companies for serious violations of fundamental human rights.[2]

I can hear the industry's leadership protesting that it cannot vet every one of thousands of exploration and extraction projects currently operating all around the globe. But this would come close to sophistry. The top men in mining (now joined by just one woman) are well aware of the allegations made against them and their fellow companies. Nor can ignorance excuse their consistent refusal to support legally enforceable sanctions against offenders, to strengthen existing initiatives and lend weight to developing ones. Of course they will continue participating in processes that they helped establish. They can rest comfortable with the Global Compact, for example, because the information they feed into its reporting procedures is little more than a carbon copy of what is already served up to their own shareholders. But when moves are afoot to strengthen procedures like the OECD Guidelines for Multinational Enterprises, it's a different story. At the root of their unease is the knowledge that 'voluntarism' (self-regulation) is increasingly under attack; after all, this is the one 'principle' to which they *have* consistently stuck for many years.

Round the tables

In 2005, an all-party Canadian parliamentary group unani-mously urged its government to introduce sanctions against companies working overseas that violate human rights norms or fail to live up to the country's social and environmental stand-ards. Although the proposal encompassed all businesses, it was clearly targeted at the extractive sector. Shortly afterwards, the Liberal federal government rejected the group's recommendations, opting instead for 'voluntary principles' and a series of nationwide 'Roundtables' . As one columnist observed, the government had bowed to 'pressure from multinational corporations [which] lobby governments furiously to ensure their rights are protected by international laws, agreements and treaties that carry serious penalties if broken – while [ensuring that] their obligations remain voluntary'.[3] In fact, the boot was firmly on both feet. For years, Canada's miners have relied on a complicit administration to provide them with a slew of subsidies, financed out of the pubic purse, both to promote investment abroad and ensure that gains come back home.[4]

Understandably the round tables have stimulated interest not only inside Canada but outside too. Should the process graduate from talking shops to the amassing of overwhelming evidence that domestic miners are violating fundamental principles, it might (just might) result in legislation. But what would new regulations actually cover? They would likely be confined to the withdrawal of government export credits, political risk insurance guarantees, tax breaks and subsidies – rather than the delisting of offenders from the country's stock exchanges, thus cutting off their equity funding. It would be a step forward but hardly a leap. Other governments have exercised similar powers in the past and only temporarily interrupted the flow of project finance. For example, the US government's Overseas Private Investment Corporation (OPIC) in 1995 withheld political risk insurance for the Lihir gold mine in Papua New Guinea. It asserted that the project's intended use of STD breached the US Foreign Assistance Act and the Federal Water Pollution Control Act, as well as two international conventions and a protocol to which the USA was a signatory. A year later, the World Bank stepped in where the US government had refused to tread[5] and the project went ahead without any alteration to the tailings disposal plan.

Relying on state intervention to bring miners to heel is rather

No means no!

181

like wielding a blunt scalpel where only a sharp instrument will do. If a community takes a company to court it stands a better chance, at least of gaining compensation for the damage it has sustained. This was illustrated by the outcome of the Yonggom villagers' case against BHPBilliton's Ok Tedi operations in Papua New Guinea (see Chapter 7), even though the out-of-court settlement did not satisfy all the claimants. Nevertheless, litigation is a slow, often frustrating process which may severely test the resilience of petitioners. In 2000, US lawyers acting for a group of Bougainville landowners filed an Alien Tort Claim suit against Rio Tinto, accusing it of 'conspiring with the Government of Papua New Guinea to quell civil resistance to an environmentally devastating copper mining operation [resulting in] actions that led to the deaths of thousands' (see Chapter 1). A Californian court sat on the documents for three years, before finally electing not to hear the case. Although it was submitted again in 2005, another fourteen months were to pass before three San Francisco judges agreed to entertain the claim. Even then, they '[left] it to Congress or the Supreme Court, to take the next step, if warranted'.[6] If and when Panguna landowners get their day in court, Rio Tinto may already be reinstated on their land.

Obtaining legal redress in South-based countries where the violations occur is even less likely to be successful. To his credit a Democratic Republic of Congo judge ruled in October 2006 that three former executives of Anvil Mining should be tried 'for war crimes' owing to the company's complicity in the Dilukushi massacre of 2004 (see Chapter 2).[7] But this was an isolated initiative. Otherwise, to quote Jamie Kneen of MiningWatch Canada:

> We know local laws don't work! Even where the laws themselves are good, enforcement is often weak and subject to corruption. Metallica Resources has been operating without a permit for over a year at San Luis Potosí in Mexico. Ascendant Copper is

violating the Ecuadorian Constitution, environmental laws, and municipal laws. Glamis Gold has been repeatedly charged with water violations in Honduras, over several years, but mysteriously not one charge has yet been heard by the courts. Bonte Gold closed its operations in Ghana in March, 2004, without giving its workers any notice or severance pay, without paying local farmers the compensation that it had agreed to for destroying their farms and orchards, and without paying the fines it owed the Ghanaian government for various spills and environmental violations.[8]

Several moves have been made in recent years to quicken the pace at which miners can be forestalled from indulging in unacceptable practices. One was launched by the small London-based Global Witness, to counter trading in 'blood' diamonds. Two more recent ones address the impacts of gold mining. In essence both seek to develop and extend the long-standing concept of 'certification'; and to varying extents both depend on collaboration from the industry.

A dead cert?

The only broadly accepted methods of certifying mining standards are those offered to businesses in general by the Geneva-based International Organization for Standardization (ISO). ISO 9000 is intended to approve a company's 'internal quality management', and ISO 14001 to confirm that a firm or project has an 'auditable environmental management system'. These certificates are proudly worn as a badge of conformity, if not excellence. They do not, however, encompass rigorous social impact assessments, while laboratory testing standards (for example, using rock samples to determine a mine's propensity to create acid drainage) may be skimped or inaccurate.[9] Customarily, monitoring visits are short, over-reliant on visual inspection and influenced by comparisons with sites that inspectors have visited

No means no!

183

before. If a 'bad' mine has already received ISO approval, then a mediocre one is also likely to do so. In 2004 I was invited by an NGO in Goa, India, to inspect an iron ore mine which, according to two groups of villagers, was contaminating a neighbouring *nulla* (stream). On presenting my evidence to the Goa State Pollution Control Board (housed in an office block owned by the biggest iron producer in Goa) that the mine was unacceptable by international standards, I was abruptly told: 'This is no concern of ours. What you have to prove is that it's worse than mines which we've already allowed to operate.' A year later, some Indian colleagues and myself visited a bauxite mine in Chhattisgarh state, where Vedanta Resources plc was anticipating an ISO visit the following day. A newly painted notice had been erected next to an unrehabilitated waste site, announcing it as a repository for topsoil with planned revegetation. In fact, most of the soil, along with bushes and trees, had long before disappeared into the mine's overburden; the dump had been hastily covered with new soil to give the pretence of a long-standing practice.

In 1992, one of the biggest and most controversial mining operations in the world was given the 'thumbs-up' by a high-level team from the International Atomic Energy Agency (IAEA), based on a five-day inspection that failed to locate important documents; nine years later the Rossing uranium mine in Namibia was granted an ISO 14001 certificate. Yet, in the interval many former miners had succumbed to cancers they believe were engendered by the conditions under which they worked and which the IAEA had woefully failed to identify (see Box 8.1)

The Global Reporting ('multi-stakeholder') Initiative (GRI) on sustainable development, floated in 1997 by CERES, embraces some aspects of certification, based mainly on reports provided voluntarily by members, rather than an independent body. In 2002 the GRI, along with ICMM, initiated a new process, further elaborated in May 2006. It was, said Paul Mitchell of ICMM, a

Box 8.1 *When an inspectorate calls*

Few people doubt that the International Atomic Energy Agency (IAEA), along with the UN Weapons Inspectorate, made a convincing job of exposing the 'prospectus' concocted by Bush and Blair to justify the invasion of Iraq in 2003. In comparison, the IAEA's earlier task of checking claims against Rio Tinto's Rossing uranium mine in Namibia left a lot to be desired. A report published in 1992 by the British Namibia Support Committee and Partizans delivered a damning indictment of conditions at the mine from its inauguration in 1976 until 1980. *Past Exposure* was based on eyewitness accounts and highly confidential documents, leaked by the Rossing mineworkers' union. It revealed appalling breaches of basic health and safety regulations. Dust levels in the open pit and ore-crushing section were nearly thirty times Rossing's official limits for respirable siliceous dust; airborne uranium concentrations came to around thirty-six times the levels imposed by the US National Academy of Sciences in 1990. It was estimated that the lifetime risk to workers of fatal cancer could be as high as 1 in 9. Moreover, a massive seepage of some 780 million gallons of radioactive liquid had continued 'as monitored by the company's own boreholes', for five years.[10] Spurred by these accusations the IAEA in 1992 sent an expert team to Rossing, which spent just five days inspecting its operations. Although conceding that there were 'serious problems with management of liquid waste', the team thereupon declared the mine to be the 'best of its kind' it had ever seen. This satisfied neither the Mineworkers Union of Namibia (MUN) nor the authors of the original report. They pointed out that, while the IAEA had gained access to some of the damning documents, by the agency's own admission, 'radiation dose records for the 1976–1980 period are unreliable or unavailable'. Yet these were precisely the years when Rossing's operations were at their most dangerous and least regulated. The inspectors did not publish (if they actually discovered) any environmental monitoring data before 1980 and, despite their avowed intention, failed to make an assessment of the long-term health effects of radiation exposure.[11]

In the fifteen years since then, the IAEA inspectorate has failed to carry out any further investigation into the Rossing mine, one of the largest of its kind.

way 'to enhance transparency in reports of companies' operations and impacts'. The CEO of GRI went a step further, claiming the process demonstrated 'an unprecedented level of transparency'. In reality the GRI flies on a wing and prayer, scarcely loftier than previous essays in the same direction and replete with good, but vague, intentions, such as 'seek[ing] continual improvement of performance' and 'contribut[ing]' to social and economic development and 'transparency engagement [sic]'.

Existing protocols designed to prevent abusive mining practices are also a form of certification. The most notable is the Kimberley Process, launched in South Africa in May 2002 to ban trade in 'conflict' or 'blood' diamonds from Sierra Leone, Angola, Côte d'Ivoire, Central Africa Republic, the two Congos and elsewhere. It has been succeeded by gambits such as the voluntary code on cyanide use and the World Gold Council's development of standards in gold manufacture (the two are closely related). Pierre Lassonde of Newmont promised in June 2006 that, through the industry-based International Cyanide Management Institute: 'We will have the gold certified by the NGOs and they will be happy that we are working to standards that they have helped set.'[12] The United Nations, the European Union, the European Commission, the World Bank/IFC, the government of Peru and the province of Ontario, Canada, have also backed the code. But, as pointed out by law professor Marcus Oreallana:

[C]ompliance is entirely voluntary and does not create enforce-able rights or obligations. ... Gold companies that become signatories to the Code are not required to have all of their opera-tions certified, only those that they have specifically requested. Independent third-party audits, including site inspections and review of records, will verify every three years whether operations meet the standards of practice and will certify compliance if war-ranted ... Operations that are only in partial compliance will be conditionally certified, subject to the successful implementation of an action plan to be posted on the Code's website. Many ques-tions remain open in the mining certification debate, such as who would set the standards and in what process; how standards would incorporate public participation and access to informa-tion; what monitoring and oversight roles [would exist] for com-munities ... [that] are wary of a tool that may serve to green-wash unfulfilled promises by an industry with a meager record of compliance and respect for human and environmental rights.[13]

With these questions going unanswered, several major NGOs have been ploughing different but converging furrows, attempt-ing to make gold mining companies more accountable. In 2001, WWF Australia started working with Barrick/Placer Dome on a pilot gold certification system.[14] Soon afterwards, Oxfam America and two other NGOs began exploring 'adequate mechanisms of community-based control, including certification' in the Andean region. In 2006, Oxfam America, WWF and Earthworks joined with global mining companies, including Newmont, BHPBilliton, Rio Tinto and Canada's Falconbridge, as well as retailers Wal-

Mart and Tiffany, to consider creating a seal of approval for 'sustainably-produced' jewellery, gold and possibly other metals.[15] The Council for Responsible Jewellery Practices has now set itself the aim of establishing a core set of social, environmental and ethical principles for the industry as a whole, covering each production stage from extraction, cutting and polishing to retail sales. Also participating in this endeavour is the Netherlands investment bank ABN Amro, which administers around a third of the £10 billion loan finance to the diamond industry.[16] It may sound promising, but as Stephen D'Esposito of Earthworks has warned: 'If the Council decides to go it alone as just companies, the only way to have legitimacy from our perspective is if they do everything right. And that's a difficult needle to thread.'[17] Raising a higher bar is Oxfam America and Earthwork's well-publicized 'No Dirty Gold' campaign, which has undoubtedly played a significant role in bringing companies and retailers to the certification table. Its demands encapsulate much of what other non-governmental and people's organizations have urged for well over a decade: endorsement of a community's right to free, prior informed consent (FPIC, sometimes called FIPC, or fully informed prior consent); rejection of riverine and oceanic waste dumping; 'no contribution to armed conflicts'; forsaking entry into protected areas; no enforced removal of local population; no 'production of uncontrolled sulphuric acid'; and the compulsory posting of corporate bonds to fund site clean-up. Several major retailers have committed themselves to complying with these objectives, sourcing gold only 'from mining operations that respect the Golden Rules', but not until 'such independently verified sources become available'. It is obvious that the more these standards are monitored by mining companies and traders themselves, then the less validity we should place upon them. But how much capacity do NGOs or governments have to take on this task themselves, and how will the monitoring be performed?

Theoretically, links in a supply or 'custody' chain should be checkable all along its trail. Nevertheless, the possibilities of diverting or 'mixing' sources are numerous. Even the Kimberley Process, adopted by a solid phalanx of companies, governments and international agencies, has failed to staunch some important leaks.[18] The Forestry Stewardship scheme to certify 'sustainable' timber production has come under fire for some of its members' recent commissions and omissions. A 2006 report by the World Rainforest Movement claimed that timber merchants in Uruguay were using a banned chemical, exhausting water supplies, failing to protect workers by granting them medical cover and implementing safety rules, while widespread planting of eucalyptus (also a favourite stand-by for 'revegetating' mine sites) was endangering soil quality.[19] Just three months later, the *Financial Times* revealed that a 'fair trade' brand of coffee was being cultivated in Peru by labourers paid less than the government minimum wage who were cultivating plants illegally in protected rainforest areas.[20] This hardly augurs well for compatible arrangements being applied to 'natural resource' extraction and sales.

Common sense tells us that observing standards at a specific mine ought to be considerably easier than following the output once it leaves the site. WWF, Greenpeace or representatives of an oversight council should be quickly able to detect illegal releases of toxic wastes into nearby rivers, or emissions of particulates under cover of darkness. On a global scale, however, this would require numerous teams of trained and fully equipped observers in attendance virtually twenty-four hours a day and with the full cooperation of the management. Even if this were practicable, these 'inspectors' could not be expected to anticipate sudden and potentially disastrous 'failures' such as those cited earlier in this book (see chapter 6). And, supposing that an operation is condemned, does this mean it will swiftly come to a close? The Ok Tedi mine was finally acknowledged to be 'not ethical' by BHPBilliton itself, after fairly rigorous independent investigation,[21] yet the mining was never even stalled. Then, in February 2002, the company transferred its 52 per cent equity to the new 'Ok Tedi Sustainable Development Program Ltd' – and withdrew.[22]

Since several metals and minerals, such as iron/steel, bauxite/aluminium, copper and coal, are produced on a huge scale, we might imagine this provides ample opportunity to track their passage all the way from minesite to the point of final offload. In contrast, illicit gems and doré gold bars may be whisked with impunity across borders and past control posts, concealed in the back of trucks or in attaché cases. Nevertheless, thousands of tonnes of coal 'disappear' each night in north-east India through the hands of the so-called 'mafia'. In 2004, an IAEA team reported that 6,000 small-scale miners had been digging up coltan (columbite-tantalite) and cobalt from the Shinkolobwe uranium mine, which was officially shut in 1960.[23] Local people forcibly reopened the site in 1997 and further attempts to seal the pits proved ineffectual. Last year, the London *Sunday Times* alleged that barrels of coltan and uranium had entered Tanzania en route to Iran.[24] These were stopped, but other consignments had doubtless got through, despite the efforts of the United Nations and the DR Congo government.

If the process of certification is to bare any teeth, the critical factor will be empowering workers and nearby communities to perform the monitoring themselves and legally empowering them to order closure. Non-governmental organizations may play a supporting role, but only under their direction.

Growing from the roots

'So what does work? Non-violent direct action and democratic decision-making!'[25]

A risk of high-profile, largely Northern-based campaigns is that they come to overshadow more locally based political actions, even though the latter may be successful while the former are not. Voters in the US states of Montana and Wisconsin, as well as in the Argentinian provinces of Rio Negro and Chubut, have been to the ballot boxes and halted the use of cyanide in gold processing. In April 2006, Turkey's Council of State annulled an earlier cabinet decree permitting cyanide to be used at a gold mine in the town of Bergama, formerly operated by Newmont. The European Court of Human Rights also sentenced Turkey to a fine of 945,000 euros in a lawsuit filed by citizens of Bergama and surrounding villages. The court's precedent-setting ruling declared that cyanidization was a violation of Article 8 (right to respect of private and family life) and Article 6 (right to a fair trial) of the European Convention on Human Rights.[26] More modest calls to outlaw the specific practice of cyanide heap leaching (the spraying of a weak sodium cyanide solution on ore exposed to the open air) feature increasingly in communities' demands and at international forums. The Czech parliament implemented such a prohibition in 1992 after Rio Tinto and Canada's TVX were pressured to relinquish two gold prospects and depart the country. Two years later, seventy-four community and NGO representatives at an International Mining Workshop, held during the last 'Prepcom' of the second WSSD, called for 'an immediate ban on destructive mining technologies, specifically open-pit mining, block-caving, cyanide heap-leaching, riverine tailing dumping, and submarine tailings disposal and a stop to uranium mining'.[27]

Obstruction of mine traffic (led more often than not by women), occupation of exploration sites and the bombardment of corporate offices are increasingly part of their direct action canon. These tactics may cost a company dear in delays to construction (time means money) or negative publicity, which hits its share price back home. Nor is it only the Bougainville islands whose use of direct action has forced an enterprise to close. Last year, when Platinex Inc. ignored a moratorium on mining activity declared by the Kitchenuhmaykoosib Inninuwug (Native Candian) First Nation in northern Ontario, the people blockaded the site and the company was compelled to withdraw.[28] In August 2006, thousands of residents and nearby villagers, including Santhal Adivsais (tribespeople), occupied the town of Phulbari, north-west Bangladesh, demanding that Britain's Asia Energy coal company should leave. A government paramilitary force attacked the demonstrators, killing six, including a fourteen-year-old boy. Revulsion spread throughout the country and the government announced a moratorium on the project – at least until the elections due in early 2007.[29]

Perhaps it is Latin American campesinos who have shown the most innovation in providing a 'demonstration effect' that might be emulated widely throughout the subcontinent.

> When Manhattan Resources wanted to displace the town of Tambogrande in northern Peru, destroying a vibrant agricultural economy to make way for an open-pit copper-gold mine, the people demonstrated against it, but they also held a referendum and voted overwhelmingly against the project. They created a crisis of democracy for a government trying to shake off a legacy of corruption, and the government had to find a way to shut the project down.[30]

In 2003 the Canadian mining company Meridian Gold bought into an open-pit mine lease several kilometres from the Argentinian city of Esquel. Learning that the company would employ cyanide in its processing, and with Meridian claiming that 'using 2,700 kilograms of cyanide a day is no riskier than driving to work' residents recruited their own mining experts.[31] Greenpeace Argentina helped commission an independent study to assess the claims made in Meridian's environmental-impact assessment. Dr

Robert Moran, a US geological and hydrological consultant from Montana, called this: 'the most "undefined" EIA I have reviewed in more than 30 years of hydrogeologic experience'. On 23 March 2003, the town held a referendum: 75 per cent of the population turned out and 81 per cent voted 'no' to the mine. According to Canadian author Naomi Klein:

> [T]hough the results of the referendum were non-binding, it served to stall the grant of permits to the company and prompted Meridian to hire the San Francisco-based Business for Social Responsibility to 'help the company listen and understand the concerns of the community'. Among BSR's findings were that the company observed a 'striking lack of consistent and comprehensive engagement' with local people.[32]

Meridian appeared to accept the criticisms, declaring that its plans were 'on pause'. It also promised not to proceed 'without the support of the Esquel community'. In the meantime, however, the company had registered a new mine lease just 4 kilometres from Esquel, thus even closer than the original one. In a late 2003 interview with Ms Klein, a Meridian spokesman crassly declared: 'Look, we're on this Earth and if it isn't growing we are going to have to mine it. ... Our entire planet has been formed on the ability of gold to form empires. Gold is a stabilizing factor throughout time.'

At the time of writing the mine was still 'on pause'. The resistance has been widely appreciated outside of Argentina (for example, being warmly received by delegates to the World Social Forum held in India in January 2004). I leave the last word with the People's Assembly of Esquel:

> This plebiscite ... shook stock markets, CEOs, and officials in Argentina, as well as in other parts of the world. It also attracted worldwide media attention. Why would this case be so significant? Because it was a simple and powerful message, not just

against the financial appetite of a particular mining company, or to reject its rather bizarre, if not sinister, digging methods. It was a public refusal of the state's mining policy. We struck a very sensitive nerve of a system that does not know how to maintain legitimacy and credibility, or how to feed the myths of 'growth' based on questionable assumptions and even more question- able consequences. The people of Esquel made visible what 'normally' is hidden from the broad public ... We refuse to accept coercion, and [we] exercise civil disobedience. No means No![33]

Notes

1 'Mining companies threaten protected forests in Indonesia', Press statement from JATAM and WALHI (Friends of the Earth Indonesia), 4 April 2002.

2 See 'Flagship or failure: the UK implementation of OECD guide- lines', published by Christian Aid, Amnesty International and Friends of the Earth, January 2006; also 'Joint NGO report on human rights and the extractive industry', published by the International Network for Economic, Social and Cultural Rights (ESCR), January 2006.

3 M. Dorhan, 'Plugging a gaping mining hole', in *Toronto Globe and Mail*, 20 October 2005.

4 J. Kuyek, *Understanding Mining Taxation in Canada*, MiningWatch Canada, Ottawa, 2004.

5 R. Moody, *The Risks We Run: Mining, Communities and Political Risk Insurance*, International Books, Utrecht, 2005, p. 203.

6 'Bougainville case against Rio Tinto set for US hearing', *Post Courier*, Papua New Guinea, 9 August 2006; 'Bougainville: islanders win court appeal', Reuters, New York, 7 August 2006.

7 K. Patterson, 'Congo wants Canadian tried for war crimes. Execu- tive, employees of mining firm "facilitated" civilian deaths, judge says', *Ottawa Citizen*, 17 October 2006.

8 J. Kneen, Presentation to the Roundtables on Corporate Social Responsibility, Montreal, MiningWatch Canada, Ottawa, 14 November 2006.

9 This test requires employing a pure form of 'reagent' water con- forming to a standard called D1193. According to one authority, D1193 'appears to be a surprisingly vague, poorly edited, error-filled, and internally inconsistent process specification ... which does not require any monitoring or maintenance of the specified purification systems ... ' See P. E. Gibbs, 'A critique of ASTM Standard D1193 Standard Specifi-

cation for Reagent Waste', American Society for Testing and Materials International, *2001 Annual Book of Standards*, vol. 11.C1, edn 2.6.

10 G. Dropkin and D. Clark, *Past Exposure: Revealing Health and Environmental Risks of Rossing Uranium*, Namibia Support Committee and Partizans, London, 1992.

11 D. Greg, 'Critique of the IAEA report on Rossing Uranium', London, 1992; *The Namibian*, Windhoek, 7 May 1993; *Parting Company*, Partizans, London, Spring 2003.

12 *Financial Times*, 28 July 2006.

13 M. Orellana, 'Certification: a field of growing trade interest', *Bridges*, CIEL, 6(4), Washington, DC, November/December 2002.

14 M. Rae and A. Rouse, *Mining Certification Evaluation Project: Independent Certification of Environmental and Social Peformances in the Mining Industry*, WWF, 2001.

15 K. Patterson, 'Miners, retailers to certify ethical production of metals. Labels on cutlery, cars, jewelry would show environmental, rights standards upheld', *Ottawa Citizen*, 14 June 2006.

16 O. Balch, 'Jewellery: industry fight to polish a flawed image', *Financial Times*, 25 November 2006.

17 Ibid.

18 See 'Conflict diamonds: agency actions needed to enhance implementation of clean diamond trade', US Government Accounting Office (GAO), Washington, DC, September 2006.

19 M. Baker, 'Forest Stewardship Council: facing a crisis of confidence?', *Ethical Corporation*, 5 June 2006.

20 '"Fair" coffee produced by underpaid workers', *Financial Times*, 8 September 2006.

21 'Ok Tedi was "not ethical"', *Post Courier*, Papua New Guinea, 15 July 2004.

22 'BHP transfers 52% to PNG company', BHPBilliton press release, 8 February 2006.

23 'DR Congo uranium mine collapses', BBC News, London, 12 July 2006.

24 'Iran's plot to mine uranium in Africa', *Sunday Times*, London, 8 August 2006.

25 Kneen, Presentation.

26 'Bergama residents win golden victory', *New Anatolian*, Ankara, 20 April 2006.

27 'Statement of the International Mining Wokshop Bali-Indonesia', Jatam, Jakarta, 24–27 May 2002.

28 Kneen, Presentation.

29 J. Doward and M. Haider, 'The mystery death, a town in uproar and US$1 UK mines deal', *Observer*, London, 3 September 2006.

30 Kneen, Presentation.

31 N. Klein, 'Once strip-mined, twice shy', *Toronto Globe and Mail*, October 2003.

32 Ibid.

33 '"IF YOU OPPOSE THE MINE, I WILL SUE YOU: the mining company takes "NO TO THE MINE" to court', Press release, People's Assembly of Neighbours of Esquel, 22 October 2006.

Appendix: the London Declaration

Taking the issues farther

The Mines and Communities network (MAC) was launched in 2001 to address all the issues covered in this book. Its guiding principles are summarized in the London Declaration (below).

Run by an editorial collective consisting of community activists from around the world, it warmly welcomes enquiries about specific campaigns and offers of support.

In the first instance, readers are invited to contact: <info@minesandcommunities.org>.

Or go to the MAC website: <www.minesandcommunities.org>.

The London Declaration

Refuting the unsustainable claims of the mining industry

Opposing current models of 'engagement'

Demanding full recognition of community rights

We – twenty-four representatives of communities and groups affected by mining from Asia-Pacific, Africa, India, South and North America – met in London from May 18–23rd 2001, to compare the impacts of mining on the lives of communities and ecosystems and to share strategies on how to confront the industry.

London is the minerals capital of the world, where a major proportion of global capital investment in mining is raised and the most active metals trading takes place. It is here that the international headquarters of some of the major mining companies are located, and that recent initiatives have been launched, seeking to persuade the 'international community' that the minerals industry can continue many of its unacceptable practices. These initiatives include the Mining, Minerals and Sustainable Development programme (MMSD) which is supported by more than thirty leading mining companies, the World Business Council for Sustainable Development (WBCSD) and the London-based International Institute for Environment and Development (IIED).

We have seen our peoples suffering for many years from mining in all stages and forms, and from exploration to development through to abandonment. Industrial mining has caused grievous pain and irreparable destruction to our culture, our identities and our very lives. Our traditional lands have been taken, and the wealth seized, without our consent or benefit.

Invariably mining imposed upon our communities has poisoned our waters, destroyed our livelihoods and our food sources, disrupted our social relationships, created sickness and injury in our families. Often our communities have been divided by 'imported' civil conflicts. Increasing mechanisation has denied many of us a role we once had as mineworkers. In recent years the mining industry has become more aggressive and sophisticated in manipulating national and international laws and policies to suit its interests. The mining laws of more than seventy countries have been changed in the past two decades. Laws protecting indigenous peoples and the environment are undermined. Structural adjustment programmes have forced many governments to liberalise capital flow for mining expansion. Their role has turned away from responsibility for the well-being of their citizens to becoming servants of the global corporations.

As a result, community resistance has significantly increased; at many sites partnerships have formed between workers and local people. In response the industry has panicked, undertaking a massive public information campaign extolling the virtues of large-scale mining, and promoting self-selected and self-regulated 'codes of conduct'.

The latest in the series of corporate-led propaganda offensives is the Global Mining Initiative (GMI), which was initially proposed by three major mining companies, and aimed at influencing the 'Rio + 10' UN World Summit on Sustainable Development, to be held in South Africa in May 2002.

The GMI has a three-pronged agenda: the self-styled research and 'dialogue' programme – Mines, Minerals and Sustainable Development (MMSD); a global conference called 'Resourcing Our Future'; and the establishment of a new international pro-mining organisation.

These initiatives promote at least four half truths or myths:

i) the supposed need for more and more minerals from ever more mines;

ii) the claim that mining catalyses development;

iii) the belief that technical fixes can solve almost all problems; and

iv) the inference that those opposed to mining mainly comprise ignorant and 'anti-development' communities and NGOs.

Our experience emphatically belies these assumptions.

We now demand the following:

1) A moratorium on new large-scale mining projects in greenfield areas of Asia, Africa and Latin America;

2) Companies must clean up the terrible damage caused by their past and current mines, without drawing on public funds, and be held morally, legally and financially responsible for their misdeeds;

3) The World Bank/IMF cease funding of industry-initiated mining codes which are imposed on the governments of Africa, Asia-Pacific and Latin America;

4) Mandatory higher standards in all mining;

5) That surface and subsurface rights of indigenous peoples and all mining-affected communities be unequivocally respected and enforced, as well as their right to veto unacceptable projects.

We seek solidarity from civil society and specifically from development and environment NGOs, in response to the global outcry from communities affected by mining. We ask these organisations:

1) To ensure that mining-affected communities are fully informed in advance on all aspects of mining and minerals projects and empowered to speak for themselves in response;
2) To refuse to participate in initiatives, such as MMSD, which are primarily spearheaded by the industry to serve its own purposes;
3) To advocate for politically and legally enforceable measures that will hold the mining industry accountable, above all to mining and exploration-affected communities.

Original signatories to the Declaration on September 20 2001 (in alphabetical order):

Armando Perez Araujo, Yanama (Colombia)

Ms K. Bhanumathi, mines, minerals and People, and Asia-Pacific Women and Mining Network (India)

Abu A. Brima, Network Movement for Justice and Development (Sierra Leone)

Ms Joji Carino, Tebtebba Foundation (Philippines) and Piplinks (England)

Catalino Corpuz, Minewatch Asia-Pacific and Tebtebba Foundation (Philippines)

Vicky Corpuz, Tebtebba Foundation (Philippines)

Abdulai Darimani, Third World Network Africa (Ghana)

Xavier Dias, mines, minerals and People (India)

Jose De Echave, Cooperacion (Peru)

Remedios Fajardo, Yanama (Colombia)

Tito Natividad Fiel, DCMI (Philippines)

Yenis Gutierrez, Yanama (Colombia)

Esther Hinostroza, Consorcio Unes (Peru)

Joan Kuyek, Miningwatch Canada (Canada)

Chalid Muhammad, Jatam (Indonesia)

Adam Rankin, Censat Agua Viva (Colombia)

Ravi Rebbapragada, mines, minerals and People (India)

Hendro Sangkoyo, Jatam (Indonesia)

Ramamurty Sreedhar, mines, minerals and People (India)

Roch Tasse, Miningwatch Canada (Canada)

Hildebrando Velez G., Censat Agua Viva (Colombia)

Jo M. Villanueva, LRC-KSK (Friends of the Earth – Philippines)

Andry Wisaya, Jatam (Indonesia)

Peter Yeboah, Wacam (Ghana)

Additional signatories (of representatives of communities and groups affected by mining from Asia-Pacific, Africa, India, South and North America):

Joan Carling, Cordillera Peoples Alliance (Philippines)

Xiong Chuhu, Hmong United Liberation Front (Laos)

Nengfue Lee, Hmong United Liberation Front (Laos)

Gabriel Rivas-Ducca, Coecoceiba-FoE Costa Rica (Costa Rica)

Bon Xiong, Hmong International Human Rights Watch (Laos)

Laura Xiong, Hmong International Human Rights Watch (Laos)

Yang, Hmong United for Freedom

Supported by:

Techa Beaumont, Minerals Policy Institute (Australia)

Frances Carr, Down to Earth: the Campaign for Ecological Justice in Indonesia (England)

Stuart Kirsch, University of Michigan (USA)

Roger Moody, Partizans (England)

Frank Nally, Society of St Columban (England)

Geoff Nettleton, Piplinks (England)

Richard Solly, Partizans (London)

Cam Walker, FoE Australia (Australia)

YOU ARE INVITED TO ADD YOUR OWN GROUP'S SIGNATURE TO THIS DECLARATION.

Please e-mail it, together with any comments or additions, to: <info@minesandcommunities.org.>

Appendix

Index

Index

The Global Issues series